From Fiji *to* America

From Fiji
to
America:

an
Immigrant Story

Jagjiwan Narayan, PhD

Cover and book design by Andy Towler
aplusscreative.com

Paperback: ISBN 979-8-9855737-0-1

eBook: ISBN 979-8-9855737-1-8

Dedicated to

My mother, Changi
&
My wife, Alexandra

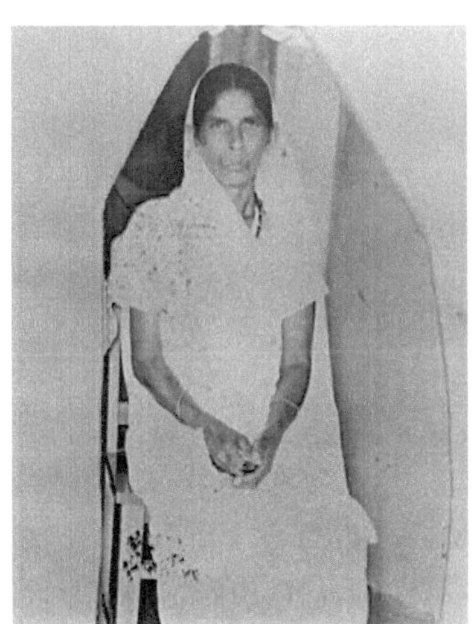

“Be a light to yourselves.
Seek no other.
Never give up.”

–Buddha’s Last Word

TABLE *of* CONTENTS

ACKNOWLEDGMENTS

I WAS INSPIRED to write my memoir, FROM FIJI TO AMERICA: AN IMMIGRANT STORY, to leave a legacy to my family and friends. I wanted to highlight the cruel history of the British Raj's Indian indenture system that my grandparents had to survive to make a better life for us. My mother Changi's courage and commitment to raising her children for success in life is remarkable and must be shared with communities everywhere.

I want to thank my second granddaughter, Kaiya Narayan, for editing the first copy of the book. Later, on my first trip to Fiji, I reviewed the memoir with my brother, Master Jai Narayan, of Jai Narayan College in Suva, Fiji. My brother suggested adding a brief history of India and the Fiji Islands to the memoir. Additionally, he wanted me to include some family history from growing up in Votualevu and in Nawaka Village, Nadi.

Last year, Yannis Peyret, now my grandson (he is married to my first granddaughter, Sasha Narayan, MD) helped me with formatting and technology. I also received much help and support from my second daughter, Tara Narayan, with editing, design, and marketing support. And most recently, I received permission from my daughter Beverly Narayan, Esq., and my wife, Alexandra Narayan.

I am deeply grateful for the help and support from my family and friends along this journey.

AUTHOR'S NOTE

AS WE BEGIN the year 2021, I would like to update you about my immediate family life. I have had a wonderful life. Let me say that both Alexandra, my wife of sixty years, and I live here in Hillsborough, California. We are both happy that our two daughters and three granddaughters are well. We are immensely proud of our family and feel so glad about their accomplishments. Most importantly, it is good to see them maintain good health and be aware of the future.

Beverly Elaine Narayan is our older daughter. Beverly was born in Berkeley, California. During this time, both Alexandra and I were on a student visa. Being on a student visa required us to be in school to remain in this country, which meant that we both had to stay in school to stay in the USA. At the time, both Alexandra and I were at Contra Costa Junior College.

Both of us had to work to pay the bills. It was a rather challenging time, especially since we needed to make sure that one of us took care of our precious child no matter the situation.

It was incredibly challenging during the school days, which meant getting Beverly to be taken care of by a babysitter. Unfortunately, she was looked after by more than a few families around our neighborhood.

Until we moved to San Francisco, her mom would take her to school around North Beach. After dropping her at the school, she would pick her up after working at the Red Cross and then take a train to come home. At the time, we lived in student housing at San Francisco State University.

Now I could work full time, and life began to improve for us. Beverly completed high school and went to SFSU for a couple of years. She transferred to the University of California, where she got her BA in political science. Beverly then started at Hastings Law School, where she earned a Juris Doctor degree. More importantly, she was able to pass the California Bar Exam on the first try. It was not easy, but our first daughter did it. Now she could practice law in the state of California. It was a proud moment for our family and friends.

I was delighted that we now had a lawyer, especially since I lost my brother Ravindra Nath, a lawyer, at a youthful age in the Fiji Islands.

Beverly is now a partner at a downtown Los Angeles law firm. Also noteworthy is that her oldest daughter, Sasha Karan Narayan, is now a medical doctor, graduating from Oregon Health and Science University with her MD. She has been accepted at Johns Hopkins University to complete her residency in psychiatry.

Her second daughter, Kaiya Maria Narayan, completed her undergraduate studies in criminal justice from The Citadel, a military college in South Carolina, where she graduated summa cum laude. She now works for the United States federal government at the Justice Department.

Our second daughter, Tara Leita Narayan, was born at Kaiser Foundation Hospital in San Francisco. Fortunately, Tara did not have to go through baby care, as did Beverly. When Tara was born, I worked for Kaiser Foundation Hospital. I also worked at French Hospital on the weekends to earn extra money. Our goal was to buy a home. We became proud owners of our new home in Daly City, California. Things were going well for us now. Alexandra was able to stay home to provide the necessary care for our little Tara. Marika, Alexandra's sister, was at our home to give us her helping hand. At the time, I worked at Kaiser Foundation Hospital, and our financial situation began to improve. It was because Alexandra had started to work for Fromm and Sichel, a wine distribution company in San Francisco. Since our life had improved, we could move out of Daly City for a better location. We wanted to be able to provide better education as well as a better environment for our two daughters.

We bought a home in Hillsborough in 1978. In retrospect, this decision was better for our family. Tara was able to complete her education in Hillsborough and later finished high school at San Mateo. She was a good student and completed her undergraduate studies at San Francisco State University with a BS degree in business administration. I remember taking her to SFSU for her orientation. I enjoyed being with Tara. I, as well, did my undergraduate degree from this university. Tara's daughter, Miss Lilou, is now in high school. We are immensely proud of Miss Lilou's academic achievement for the first semester of 2021, with a 3.91 GPA. Of the eleven classes, she has ten A's and one B.

Alexandra and I continue to live here in Hillsborough. As stated earlier, we are starting a new year under a new administration. Our country is under tremendous pressure due to the Covid-19 pandemic. This situation is not limited to the USA but exists throughout the world. So far, we are doing well, and I am thankful for our family support. Alexandra and I try to manage our life together.

PREFACE

October 27, 2020

I AM NOW an old man, and the last child of my mother, Changi. My mother, Changi, a first-generation Fiji-Indian woman, was married at age thirteen to Baijnath of Votualevu. It is common for Indian girls to be married at a youthful age. My mother and Baijnath lived in Votualevu, working their land farming sugarcane and other crops. They were happily married and had five children between them. The children's ages were from eight years to four months of age when Baijnath suddenly passed away. My mother became a widow at the age of twenty-three when Baijnath died. My mother was devastated as was the rest of the family. Her father, Ram Phal, wanted her to return to his home, which she refused to do. Mother Changi was determined to raise her children for success in life despite facing tremendous difficulties. However, she was forced to send a few of her older children to her parents' home, which was in Nadi Town.

After Baijnath's sudden death, his younger brother and my father, Jai Karen, became intimately involved with my mother. Although my father already had a wife and six children, the Indian culture required Baijnath's brothers to care for his now-widow and children. My father and mother had three of their own children, including me, so my mother now had eight children to care for. Money had been borrowed to keep the sugar cane farm going, but because the creditors ultimately could not be repaid, my mother's home and sugar cane farmland in Votualevu had to go on the auction block. With nowhere to go, and my mother's father having gone to India, my grandmother loaned her daughter 900 pounds to buy land in Nawaka Village. The entire family then moved to Nawaka Village to begin a new life there.

This book tells the story of my family, both past and present. It tells about my grandparents, taken from British India to Fiji to work as Girmitiyas, supposed contracted laborers but treated as slaves. It tells of past suffering but exposes the Girmitiya system to be alive and well in the present.[1] It tells of my grandparents' and their first-generation children's sacrifices to create a better life for their families. And it tells of my mother and extraordinary woman, Changi, a child of Girmitiyas, who faced incredible challenges but was determined that all her children would succeed and thrive in life.

1 Fiji Indians cannot own Fiji land, they can only lease it. Fiji's tribal chiefs can seize Fiji land, and everything on it, at any time.

PART I:

THE HISTORY *of* MY FAMILY

Chapter 1

THE BEGINNING

MY GRANDPARENTS BEGAN their life in Fiji in the late 1800s. The Indian indentured labor system started in 1879 when Sir Arthur Gordon became governor of Fiji[1]. In the years between 1879 to 1916, up to 60,553 Indian laborers were brought to Fiji[2]. It was because there was a massive shortage of labor needed for the sugarcane plantations. India was the perfect source for this labor. First, most of the Indians recruited for Fiji already did farming in India for their subsistence. Secondly, Indians are the most hard-working ethnic group, especially the Vaishya and the Shudra cast. While visiting India, I saw sugarcane farming alive in Uttar Pradesh. In India, UP is the largest producer of sugarcane. During the forty years of indenture, a total of eighty-seven of what were then called "Coolie ships," a derogatory term, were used to transport these laborers. From the very start, it was made clear that the indentured laborers would work for a minimum of five years under a special labor contract[3].

Sir Arthur Gordon was the perfect person since he had experience with Indian indentured laborers in Trinidad and Mauritius. Her Majesty Queen Victoria handpicked Sir Arthur Gordon to be the first governor of Fiji. He was fully aware of Indians' capacity for demanding work. In fact, of all those recruited to work in Fiji, Indians proved to be better workers than any other group. Another reason for recruiting Indians was that India was at the time a sub-continent of the British Empire[4]. My maternal grandfather, Ram Phal, was from Basti, Siddharthnagar. I was fortunate to meet him as a young boy while growing up in Fiji. My paternal grandfather, Shiugahan, was from the western Indian state of Bihar. Unfortunately, I did not get to meet him. My Aji (paternal grandmother) came from Allahabad in the northern Indian state of Uttar Pradesh. Unfortunately, no one in our family has much information about her.

Uttar Pradesh is the most populous, and poorest, state in India. As of 2019, it remains the most impoverished state in India. However, Uttar Pradesh was home to the most powerful emperor of medieval and ancient India. The state, whose capital is Lucknow, has some of the holiest Hindu temples and pilgrimage centers. Some of the other important cities are Agra, Varanasi, Ayodhya, and Gorakhpur. Kanpur, a metropolitan city in Uttar Pradesh state, was one of the most crucial for the British Raj. It was because of the military as well as being a commercial center for the British Empire

The British Raj created Uttar Pradesh as the most populous state in India because of its history and some very well-known towns and cities. It became abundantly clear that those recruited for migration to Fiji were from poor villages in India. There is no reason to deny that many people who remained poor around the towns in India were very susceptible to getting recruited. It is essential to recognize that the state was known for its sugar industry, although it has changed now to the service industry. Once they arrived in Fiji, most of these people settled in Ba, Fiji. Here they all served their indentured period for five years as per the agreement. The agreement was a binding contract that they had to sign or put their thumb mark on showing that they had agreed to leave India. Of course, since they did not speak any English, probably, they did not know or understand the content of the contract.

After serving their time of five years, they were free and had three options. Option one was that they could return to India after the five-year contract expired. Those who had the money to buy their passage chose to go back to their homeland of India. Option two was to get re-indentured to their old plantation or renew the contract for another five years. Those who served for ten years were entitled to free passage to India. Some decided to take advantage of this option. Those who did decide on this option were strong and did not mind the rigorous work they demanded on the plantation. The work included weeding along the cane line, using hoes 1,200 to 1,300 feet long (about the height of the Empire State Building) and six feet wide. It was known as "full task" hard labor[6]. Sources point out that the laborers had difficulty finishing the work assigned and thus got punished in most cases. In addition to the job, these laborers faced harassment by the Sardars regularly. The Kolumber (white leaders) handpicked the Sardars. The Sardars regularly beat, kicked, and whipped the workers. This harassment took place while they worked extremely hard under a hot sun for long hours. They were required to work for five and a half days per week for a mere one shilling per day. They had to complete the assigned task, and when they could not complete the job, they were beaten and got reduced pay for the day.

The third option was having served for five years, one could remain in Fiji and become independent and work on their farm. Most of the indentured workers chose this option, including my grandparents. Here they were allowed to lease from the Fijian government or the planters and make Fiji their home[7].

My Aji (grandmother) married my Aja (my paternal grandfather Shiughan from Arrah) while they were serving their five-year contract in Ba. Having completed work for five years, they decided to remain in Fiji and make their home there. If they had worked as indentured laborers for another five years, would they have returned to their home in India? The government would have paid for their passage back to India, including their children's. Did the government share this critical information with the laborers? However, like many others, they chose to remain in Fiji as indentured laborers.

After serving the Girmit (agreement), they needed to survive and make a better life for themselves and their children as they were the first generation in the Fiji Islands. I am pleased about the choice they made for us, it is because they assured that their life and the life of future generations would be prosperous and productive in Fiji.

They settled in Votualevu, which was close to the Nadi airport. Their married life was a happy one despite numerous challenges they faced as a young couple. The Shiugahan's had four children, three sons and one daughter. Baijnath was the eldest son, the second son was Jai Karan, and the third son was Bal Karan. The couple's daughter was named Shewraji. It was apparent that their life together was a healthy and happy one. Once free of their indentured servitude, they were hopeful that they would improve their living conditions with demanding work.

When visiting Ba today, it is easy to see the fruits of their labor and the industry of free settlers, laborers who decided to remain in Fiji. They made their lives a real success. Many of us are privileged today because of these Girmitiyas. Girmitiyas, also known as Jahajis, were the indentured laborers (a person doing unskilled manual work) for wages who signed a contract to work in Fiji for five years. Upon visiting India, it is apparent that those Girmitiyas, who risked everything to come to Fiji, did have a better life than if they had remained in India, it is because of the lack of opportunity with village life. However, it was not easy toiling the land from sunset to sundown, for five and a half days per week for a pittance. Those Girmitiyas who survived the hardship and cruelty of their masters should make us proud of their perseverance. Those of us who are the children of the Girmitiyas should never forget the hardships and suffering of our ancestors.

I did not live in Ba, nor do I live in Fiji any longer because of the many difficulties we Indians have to bear in Fiji. One of the significant issues facing Indians in Fiji is the land situation. Who is the beneficiary of the Fijian land that is divided into three parts: freehold land, crown land, and native lease land.[8] The Fijians owned up to eighty percent of the land. Thus, for an Indian farmer to cultivate such land, they must get the lease from the Fijian owner. The farmers who lease these lands work hard to feed their families. Farmers face many difficulties during the time they occupy Fiji land. First, they are required to plant sugarcane to get the lease. Sugarcane farming for the owner is where he gets cash. It is not easy to cultivate the land for sugarcane farming, however. It is tough being a farmer because all work is manually done and relies heavily on having bullocks or horses to help with making the land arable for planting sugarcane.

Depending on the type of land, it was acceptable to plant rice. For a rice plantation, the ground must be exceptionally soft, meaning that it should have lots of water, unlike for sugarcane planting, where the soil must be dry. For subsistence, it waspermissible to have a vegetable garden. It was customary practice while I was growing up in Fiji. With vegetable gardening, when there was excess, we used to take it to the Nadi market to generate some cash.

Fiji Island is prosperous and thriving today because of the indentured laborers who came from India. The Indian population has decreased by large numbers. At one point, the Indian population increased rapidly and by 1965 reached up to fifty-one percent of the total population. However, there was a dramatic decline after 1970, primarily due to migration. This migration was caused by instability within Fiji's governing system. The first coup of 1987 caused most of the Indians to leave Fiji. Countries such as New Zealand and Australia opened their borders for those Indians who wanted to migrate. Unfortunately for Fiji, those who were going were the most educated and prosperous. Those who stayed back mainly were poor farmers.

Indians cannot own much land, especially in areas made arable by our Girmitiyas family. Since the Fijians own up to eighy percent of the land, the Indian farmers must lease from indigenous Fijians. The lease is for thirty years to Indian farmers. Irene Jai Narayan (my sister-in-law) was the president of the National Federation Party. The parliament of Fiji had a much-heated dialogue on managing land leasing to the Indian farmers. The land situation remains a significant issue in Fiji. The indigenous Fijians take over the land upon the expiration of the lease. This system is accelerated since there is extraordinarily little to not much support provided by the Fijian government. Ironically, those Girmitiyas who cleared the land for sugarcane farming had to get the leased land without much guarantee for their future.

On my recent visit to Fiji, it was apparent that not much has progressed about Fiji's land situation. It has become worse than my first return trip to Fiji in 1967. I saw lots of lands once covered with sugarcane now lying idle. It is regrettable to see these cane fields now with lush grasses rather than sugarcane. In some cases, people have built their homes on the land as well. The native Fijians, in most cases, are not interested in sugarcane farming. It was apparent to me while I was growing up in Fiji, and it has remained the same even now.

In many cases, the landowners, the iTaukei (indigenous people of Fiji), have seized the lands from the Indian farmers and have not made any effort to cultivate them. They seem more interested in occupying the homes vacated by the Indian farmers. It is also evident that Fijians who once lived in village communities generally no longer wish to live there since they can quickly move into a home occupied by Indians. One undeniable and depressing result has been that most of the original settlers who made Nawaka Village (my birthplace) a lively and flourishing village have been forcibly removed. Although Nawaka had little to offer economically, the people's needs were limited, and they lived there happily. I once worked here on our farm and provided support to my family. My family depended on the land to provide us with income and food items as needed. Not only did we cultivate the land with sugarcane farming, but we also planted rice, corn, beans, and more. I do have some fond memories of my days in this village life. I was only thirteen years of age then and worked on the farm till the age of seventeen. One of the primary reasons for my not going to high school was that two of my brothers were in India for their university education. The third one had gone to New Zealand for his university education. All Fiji high school graduates needed to go overseas for undergraduate studies since, at the time, Fiji did not have universities.

It was widespread practice by the Arkatis (agents who helped to recruit indentured laborers in India) to get as many young men and women from different villages in India as possible to work in Fiji. Both our maternal and paternal grandfathers came from different district of India. Ram Phal, my maternal grandfather, was from Uttar Pradesh, the village of Kabolia near Naugarh in the district of Siddharthnagar. I learned later that he was already married in India and had a daughter there. It isn't easy to find out about his wife and daughter in India. Once in Fiji, he remarried Sitlee, an indentured laborer who came from a village close to the city of Allahabad in Uttar Pradesh. After completing their indenture period, they settled in Nawaka, and all their children were born there. My maternal grandfather's seven children—three sons and four daughters—were born in Nawaka, Nadi. My mother, Changi, was the eldest of all the children.

Our family life in Fiji began at the Nawaka village. It is intriguing that our grandparents left India from different states and met up in Fiji to start their families.

The Gupta Empire also was known as the Golden Age of India[9]. It is interesting to note that the Gupta Empire was around after the death of Christ—a long time ago. There was extensive innovation, invention, and discovery in science and technology, logic, mathematics, astronomy, and engineering. The king at this time was Chandra Gupta I. He established his empire around 320 CE[10]. On the other hand, Chandra Gupta Maurya founded the Mauryan Empire. The Mauryan Empire existed before Christ[11].

Chandra Gupta Maurya was recognized as the most powerful king. He led India during the sixth century BCE. During his time, India controlled landmass from Nepal to Afghanistan. His kingdom was significant and influential, for there continue to be his memories of his legacy to this day. His offspring continued to dominate India for many years. Chandra Gupta Maurya founded the Gupta Empire and got credited for unifying most of India under one administration.

Chandra Gupta's son, King Asoka, established a democratic government before Western civilization recognized its benefits. It is interesting for me to learn that Chandra Gupta married a Greek princess, and some believe that his grandson may have had some Greek blood. His son may also have been able to speak some Greek. I do not wish to compare, but I have also been married to a Greek woman for over sixty years. King Asoka was the greatest ruler in Indian history. He was generous in creating a society where people mattered. He provided free healthcare and made sure that there was schooling and a support system for his citizens.

In terms of religion and belief by the majority, it is interesting to note that the Mauryan Empire promoted non-Hindu religion, while the Gupta Empire promoted Hinduism. My maternal grandfather's family in India have adopted the name Maurya. I am not able to confirm that they are from the Maurya clan. It is significant to look at what prompted our family to migrate to Fiji. Primarily they were deceived, tricked by the Arkatis or the recruiters. Of course, they promised that there would not be any suffering and that there would be plenty of food like bananas and sugarcane to eat. Finally, they would get 12 annas (1/16th of a rupee or 0.013 of a dollar) per day. All were promises that they would earn lots of rupees in Fiji, and after five years, they would all return to India a wealthy person[12].

The sailors that brought the indentured laborers to Fiji was not concerned about their cargo of human beings, nor did they care about the traditional backgrounds of the people on the ship. There was no distinction between the castes of the people on the vessel. The Chamar, Brahman, Sikhs, Rajputs, Chris, Koli, etc., had to be treated in the same manner[13]. The positive side of this situation, in some cases, led to real bonding among some, known as jahaji bhai. I remember my maternal grandfather's jahaji bhai, who lived in Suva, the capital city in Fiji.

A male doctor would perform the medical exam on these

people before they boarded the ship. I can just imagine the type of examination conducted on these people, especially since most were young. The doctors similarly examined both men and women. Each person got a tin jar for water, a tin plate for food, and a small sack for keeping any belongings. They wore unique clothes while on the ship[14]. The sailors' only interest was to deliver the human cargo to Fiji. It mattered little to them who these people were, their caste, or their ways of life. Delivering this human cargo was a priority, and nothing was going to stop them.

The man and women on the ship were from many levels of society. These Indians were needed as laborers to cultivate the land in Fiji. Their passage was arduous, especially since most of the passengers on the ship had never seen such a massive amount of blue seawater or "Kala Pani" in their life. Many people died from diseases such as typhoid, cholera, and others that were often difficult to diagnose. The food preparation did not meet the standard these people were used to in their villages. Thus, malnutrition was evident all around them.

In many cases, vegetarian people could not eat meat, which led to weakness and anemia. The causative agent for tuberculosis and leprosy is the genus of bacteria known as Mycobacterium. Some decided to commit suicide due to the unacceptable conditions on the ship. The conditions on board the vessel were intolerable. The people were huddled together in groups. All felt cloistered and that they were in cage-like states. There was total disregard for families. Many felt alone and discouraged, longing to go back to India. But it was too late! That was because they already had signed a legal document for departing India for a minimum of five years per contract agreement. The journey was long, tiring, and depressing. They spent many sleepless nights. Misery was all around them, and the future appeared to be grim. They did not have any choice with whom they could associate as they had in India. There was no choice in this situation but to be housed with outcasts or "untouchables," thus, creating further hardship for the individuals and their families. The ship's captain and crew had total control over the human cargo and did not understand their needs. Their marching orders were to deliver all on board safely regardless of the health and desires of the individuals.

Aside from people's traditions and customs, food was another major problem. The ship's food was prepared in bulk and did not meet their needs. In many cases, it was unacceptable. It was never the case in their village life in India. However, one favorable effect of this was that it was the beginning of losing their caste division. Now in Fiji, the caste divisions of Indians are outdated. The people do not know the caste system as it is in India. It is good that we do not force humans to divide into groups not of their own choice forcefully.

There was rampant cholera on the ship. It was due to the lack of proper hygiene and unfamiliarity with the surroundings. It is also true that when people are huddled closely together, they can spread several types of diseases. Besides, they suffered from all sorts of sicknesses from the start. Of course, the sanitation on the ship was not up to par. How were those used to managing their waste products in the fields expected now to use Western styles of sanitation? So, the long journey to Fiji proved difficult and painful for the indentured laborers and often fatal.

Chapter 2

A BRIEF HISTORY *of* INDIA

INDIA IS A country with a vibrant history and culture of which we Indians are enormously proud. Even though it faced many invaders during its existence, it never once tried to inflict harm on anyone. Its civilization gave rise to people with highly advanced knowledge of the universe. It is a country known for its great traditions, rich culture, and philosophy. History teaches us that India distinguishes itself from others in that it has never conquered another country and was ruled over several times by other countries. One of the well-known examples is the British Raj.

Most importantly, Indians believe in a life that does not cause harm to anyone, including animals. Its religion is all about tolerance. Many believe India's religion, when appropriately translated, is a way of life. It accepts all religious beliefs. For example, being an Indian, I feel extremely comfortable going to any church, temple, mosque, or gurdwara and embracing preaching without prejudice. This type of thinking makes India out to be a country of peace-loving people.

India became a free nation from the British Raj on August

15, 1947. However, its history goes back thousands of years. The British ruled India for two hundred years.[1] Some people think that this is a myth. It should be only one hundred years because it took one hundred years to conquer India. The country is truly diverse, and the people are incredibly inventive as well as highly creative. Indian society includes five hundred castes and communities, each with its customs and traditions. It is a country known to many as a world of miracles. Some believe that India gave birth to two of the oldest religions practiced in many countries today. India is highly tolerant of other religious faiths. There are more Muslims in India than in many other countries. India has welcomed Jews and Parsees as refugees. Even today, India welcomes refugees from other nearby countries. One good example is Tibet, as the Dalai Lama and many of his followers live in India. All this I observed personally during my visit to India in 2010.

I am intrigued by India as having an Aryan civilization. The word Aryan means the noble ones. They are primarily in northern India. Their contribution to India is enormous. It is because they created two of the greatest epics in Indian history—the *Ramayana* and the *Mahabharata*, the two religious books part of all Hindu life. Thus, the Indians regard themselves as belonging to the Aryan race. Hitler claimed that Germans were Aryans. India has asserted that right first, and therefore it is a truism that the Aryan language of Sanskrit made it possible for India to be a nation where Aryans thrived. Sir

William Jones, a Welshman, and a British judge in Kolkata, was a brilliant linguist who knew Greek, Latin, and Persian, and announced to a newly formed Asiatic Society of Bengal on February 2, 1786, his discovery about Sanskrit:

> *"The Sanskrit language, whatever be its antiquity, is of wonderful structure; more perfect than the Greek, more copious than the Latin, and more exquisitely refined than either—yet bearing to both of them a stronger affinity, both in the roots of verbs and in the forms of grammar, than could have been produced by accident. So strong indeed, that no philosopher could examine them all three without in them to have sprung from some common source, which, perhaps, no longer exists."*[2]

It is no coincidence that Jones appeared on the scene in India at this time, for India was trying to find out about the Aryan nation and the origin of Rig-Vedic people[3].

The history of India and its people is extraordinarily complex. There are many books on the language and people. Rig-Veda and the other three Vedas, Sama Veda, Yajur Veda, and Atharva Veda, were passed on by word of mouth initially. It took ten years for a student to learn all this by heart. Thus, they were passed on from one generation to another until all got put in writing. The Brahmin families were the only group that received these sacred books. For more than two thousand years, they got transmitted orally. The first text was written in the Middle Ages on a palm leaf and later paper. Those persuaded to leave India took such traditional and rich culture to Fiji, a land unknown to them where, in the 1800s, cannibalism was even practiced[4]. Of course, those selected to live in Fiji did not have much education or opportunity for schooling in the villages in India. Thus, in any case, they were given false promises and deceived by the Arkatis, the licensed recruiters for migration.

The Aryans were instrumental in creating an agricultural society. They armed the warrior class and upheld the idea of class differentiation. They made the three-tier division of society: priests, warriors, and farmers. Below them were the workers, servants, and slaves who came from the majority indigenous population. Here lies the root of the caste system in India. This caste system later used verna (color) and jati (literally "births,") for the level of society or rites as the critical definers of individuals. In this case, Hindu practices include rituals such as puja (prayer service) and other solemn ceremonies or acts. It is worth it for me to recognize the significant role of the *Mahabharata* and the *Iliad*. The *Mahabharata* is sometimes called the Greek Epic of India. Just like Homer's *Iliad*, the tale of Troy became a defining text of Greek culture.

Both have some similarities, and both cultures taught us about civilization with many roots in our modern world. For example, I met and married a Greek woman, not knowing these historical significances. For me, it is essential to point out that I was born in the Fiji Islands. My mother was a first-generation woman born in the Fiji Islands. She was a child born of an indentured laborer, my maternal grandfather, who was brought to Fiji from India in 1902. I often joke to my Greek family about our Indian roots in that the Greeks may have copied much material from India.

Chapter 3:

A BRIEF HISTORY *of* FIJI ISLANDS

FIJI IS WELL known by many, for the new day begins here: Fiji Islands, located in the southwest Pacific Ocean. When one looks for Fiji on the world map, one will find a tiny dot. In terms of location, it is 2,797 kilometers (about half the width of the United States) northeast of Sydney, Australia, and 1,848 kilometers (about the distance from Florida to New York City) north of Auckland, New Zealand. The 180 degree meridian runs close to Vanua Levu, the second-largest island of the group of 300 islands, and 540 islets scattered over about 1,000,000 square miles (about the area of India), of which fewer than 100 are inhabited. Abel Tasman, a Dutch explorer, first discovered Fiji in 1743, then it was discovered later by English explorers, Captain James Cook in 1774, Captain Wilson in 1779, and Captain William Bligh in 1789[1]. It is interesting to note that the first Europeans to land on the island and live with the Fijians were convicts who escaped from Australia. These Australians were able to live among the native Fijians without any difficulty.

Ratu Seru Cakobau of the Bau ruled Fiji at the time. There

used to be lots of infighting among the chiefs during that time. Ratu Cakobau won the fight with Kab and proclaimed himself the paramount chief. He later claimed the title of Tui Viti or the king of Fiji[2].

Vanua Levu is the second-largest island, located northeast of Viti Levu. European traders had good knowledge regarding sandalwood, including its location. I happen to have a large piece of sandalwood given to me by my sister-in-law, Irene Jai Narayan. Vanua Levu also has a large coconut plantation.

The third-largest island is Taveuni, located to the east of Vanua Levu. Taveuni is well known for scuba diving. A few of my friends from California have gone there to scuba dive. Kadavu lies to the south of Viti Levu and is the fourth-largest island in the archipelago. This island is reputed to be the center of traditional Fijian culture and is often not seen by tourists.

The largest island is Viti Levu. The capital city is Suva, the largest city, the chief port, and the capital. The second-largest city is Lautoka, the second port of entry. Nadi is the site of the international airport, the largest on the Fiji Islands[3].

The original inhabitants may have come from the southeast via Indonesia. Fiji is a meeting place of Polynesian and Melanesian cultures. These two groups melded together to create a highly developed society in Fiji. The two major ethnic groups are the "iTaukeis," (the native Fijians) and the Indians. At one time, the Indian population had reached fifty-one percent. The total now is reduced to about thirty-two percent, primarily due to emigration to England, Canada, the United States, Australia, and New Zealand. The decrease in the Indian population is due to the coup of May 19, 2000. A shameful event! It was George Speight who led the coup in 2000. Speight was an educated man, holding bachelor's and master's degrees in business administration. One of the primary reasons for the coup was that the prime minister was an Indian man, Mr. Mahendra Chaudhry. The bottom line is that the indigenous Fijians did not wish to have any other group governing other than them.

The Europeans first came to Fiji to obtain sandalwood, which grew wildly in Bua Bay in Vanua Levu. There was great demand first in India and China, and they paid unreasonable prices for it. When the sandalwood trade died down due to a lack of trees, the trade in bêches-de-mer (sea cucumber) became more prominent, thus opening up opportunities for sailing ships. When these sailing ships noticed large whale populations, it was not long before Fiji became the center of the whaling trade.

In 1874, Fiji became part of the British Empire. In the beginning, the European planters, who came to own large estates, grew cotton profitably. However, when the cotton price declined in the world market, the trade declined, and the planters began to grow other crops commercially.

Sugarcane was grown in Fiji before the first Europeans arrived. Some planters experimented with the crop, and it became apparent that sugarcane could be quickly grown in the flatland areas of the country. Small sugar mills got established in the country, which laid the foundation of the Fijian sugar industry.

Earlier labor for cotton plantations was met by laborers forcibly brought from other islands of the Pacific, particularly from the Solomon Islands. These laborers got kidnapped from these islands. Once the kidnappers owned these souls, it was easy for them to be sold to the planters in Fiji and the other places where there was a demand for labor.

When Fiji came under British rule (1874 to 1970), the corrupt system of getting laborers from the islands stopped. Sir Arthur Gordon, then the governor of Fiji, did not want to break up the village life of the native Fijians and destroy their communal living situations. He had seen that the indentured system had worked successfully in Trinidad and Mauritius and decided to introduce the same approach in Fiji.

The first batch of Indian laborers arrived in Fiji in 1879. Between 1879 and 1916, a total of 60,553 indentured laborers got recruited from India[4]. These indentured workers were required to work nine hours per day for five and a half days per week. The agreement was that the laborers would return to India after serving in Fiji for five years at their own expense. However, if they served for another five years, the Fijian government paid their passage and their children. Most of the laborers did not come willingly. The recruiting agents in India tricked most of the potential workers into coming to Fiji. However, for some, the living standard in India was also a factor in them wanting to migrate.

This was true for the untouchables, who came by choice.

It is difficult to imagine people's life on the plantation. At a minimum, it had to be extremely complicated. The housing of laborers was in "lines:" rows of long barracks, each containing sixteen rooms, measuring three meters by three and a half meters, each room housing either three single men or a married man with his wife and three children. They earned a shilling a day if they completed the task assigned to them. However, if they failed to complete their work, they were denied any payment. Abuses and beatings were common. Some could not endure the suffering and became victims of the system and died. Most of the Indians who came to Fiji were from eastern Uttar Pradesh and western Bihar. Approximately seventy-five percent of Indians came to Fiji from Kolkata and the rest of them from Madras. These were of South Indian descent, also recruited during the later years of the indenture system. The Gujarati were latecomers. They, along with the Sikhs, came after the labor system. The Gujarati were primarily interested in the shopkeeping business.

All Indians in Fiji speak "Fiji Hindustani," a dialect that is a mixture of Hindi, English, and some Fijian. They continue to mostly maintain their religion and village culture, which their ancestors brought with them. However, things like giving a dowry during marriage or giving unequal status to women are things of the past. Due to their sufferings, both sexes quickly recognized the value of education and made sure that their children got educated.

When the social evils of the indentured system became known in India, Indian leaders like Gokhale, Gandhi, and C. F. Andrews fought for its abolition. The recruiting stopped in 1916, and by 1920, the system was utterly abolished[5]. It was because that existing contract was to end on January 1, 1920.

After completing their indentured period, most laborers decided to remain in Fiji rather than India. They mostly became small tenant farmers, leasing small pieces of land from the native Fijians.

Of course, this was not the promise made while being recruited from different villages in India. All were in the dark about their destination—promised wealth, a better life, freedom, and only a five-year contract. At the end of five years, all would return to their home in India as wealthy people. No one became wealthy; however, some decided to leave Fiji, but there were very few. Many feared returning to India and not being accepted by their families especially if they did not have much contact with their families in India while they were in Fiji for five years.

These were the people who defended India with their lives to maintain their lifestyle and way of life. The British Empire ruled India during this time; it is not difficult to see their will to recruit many with lofty promises. They also knew that for them to manage the colonies, laborers would be needed.

After the abolition of slavery in 1833, it became necessary to meet the demand for labor in the colonies. The British government planned to meet this demand by getting laborers from India under what came to be known as the "indenture system." The colonial government of India passed Act V of 1837. This act was significant in that it created the essential mechanism and the regulatory framework of the system as follows:

> *"The intending immigrant must appear before an officer designated by the Government of India. He was also required to produce a written statement of the terms of the contract. The length of service was to be five years, renewable for further five-year terms. The emigrant must return at the end of his service to the port of departure. The vessel taking the emigrants was required to conform to specified standards of space, diet, etc. Each ship was required to carry a medical man to care for the coolies."*[7]

While it is an excellent idea to establish reasonable guidelines, it needs to follow the proper protocol.

It seems clear that no one person was responsible for overseeing that established procedure. The system worked well in the West Indies (Trinidad, Guinea) and Mauritius, and Sir Arthur Gordon, the governor of Fiji, decided to bring the laborers from India when the demand for labor grew.

The Indian migration to Fiji began in 1879. Sir Gordon was responsible for making the migration possible. The first ship, *Leonidas,* brought 464 Indians to Fiji on May 18, 1879[8]. It was essential to keep the new arrivals at a quarantine station for surveillance as to their condition. They were held at Nukulau Island, close to Suva, the capital of Fiji. Each person required a physical examination. This was done to check an individual's physical condition, for employability. Those individuals who were unfit had to go back immediately to India. During this period, life for indentured people in Fiji was not conducive to creating a civilized society. Many indentured laborers called it a Narak, or "hell on earth."[9]

My maternal grandfather arrived in Fiji in 1902, and my paternal grandfather arrived in Fiji in 1894. During this time, the life of indentured peoples had begun to improve.

According to some writers, the improvement of indentured lives was due to pressure from India. India was still under British rule, and people like Gandhi, C. F. Andrews (a close friend of Gandhi's), and others worked hard to improve the living conditions of Indian laborers in Fiji.

Their efforts helped abolish the indenture system in 1966. Indians were British citizens, thus there was more reason to treat them with fairness. However, the British were known to be highly prejudicial toward Indians and, in fact, to people who were not white. It was not difficult to persuade, coerce, lie, and, if necessary, force innocent people to sign a document or place a thumbprint if they were illiterate. The record was a piece of paper that was an agreement, also known as Girmit, by our Indian brothers. Once they signed or put their thumb impression, it sealed their future. This agreement contained the terms and conditions of employment. At the time, it was no other than the British government that created the agent system. Because of this system, it was easy to send the laborers to Fiji, Mauritius, Guyana, Suriname, and a few other countries as a British subject. It was "Girmit"[10].

The majority of those who signed the document were village people, mostly young men under twenty. Some were older, including women and children who got caught in this web. It was apparent that most were not very educated and thus got lost in their own country. Thus, they were ripe for the picking by the Sardar (a general or chief). These were the people who were hired by the British to find young men for the indentured system. Many have tried to discover how this could have happened to the Indian people. Many have written books on the subject, and it is difficult to discern the truth. That said, it is clear the reason in many cases was to find a better life for those who decided to take the risk. But more importantly, they were coerced and persuaded to sign because of the false promise of a better life. India, as we know, is an emerging country and, even then, it was not difficult to find those who wanted a better life.

Chapter 4

MATERNAL *and* PATERNAL GRANDPARENTS

SHIUGAHAN, MY AJA (my paternal grandfather), arrived in Fiji in 1894 and settled in Votualevu after serving his Girmit in Ba. According to my brother, Master Jai Narayan, our Aja was very dynamic. He was determined and visionary and recognized the future with enthusiasm. He had the foresight to see how farming sugarcane could make the family succeed in life. In fact, upon review of his emigration pass, he was identified as belonging to Koiri, an Indian caste. This caste is found in Bihar, recognized as cultivators. Having such a background and given his twenty-three years, he decided to invest in farming land and bought thirty acres of fertile area in Votualevu. As in any family, it is about leadership and having someone in the family to take charge. Proper education is essential for the family, especially the women, to be part of any endeavor. A Fakir Lala from India tutored his eldest son, Baijnath, and his other two sons in Hindi. His sons, Baijnath, Jai Karan, and Bal Karan, were fortunate to have such enthusiastic parents and had the best land. Shiugahan was the leader in his community and was admired by many for his intellect.

He was well respected and admired because of his many leadership qualities. He learned to read and write, which was a gift under the indentured system. Among Indian culture, we know that the oldest son carries a heavy burden, because he becomes the family's caretaker in case of the death or illness of the parents. Baijnath was a physically strong man and well versed in the Hindi language. He was highly regarded and was looked up to by the members of the community. I understand he had great strength and thus was called a "bully," a name his friends gave for strength and intellect. Bal Karan was not interested in farming. He was an exceptionally talented musician; he mostly played the dholak (a double-headed cylindrical drum), and he was interested in black magic. During this time, it was in high demand within this poor community of indentured Indians. He was astute and wrote his songs. Because of his interest in music, he was always away from home and not around the family to help. But Jai Karan, my father, showed some interest and thus ended up doing most of the work at the sugarcane farm, which kept our family together. All Shiugahan's sons were gifted intellectually. It was evident by their ability to learn Indian religious books. My father, Jai Karan, had memorized many extracts of the *Mahabharata*, a well-recognized holy book in the Hindu religion. Indeed, this was not an easy task for any ordinary man to do. The famous Hindu epic is said to be longer than *The Iliad*. Both *Mahabharata* and *Ramayana* are the two major Sanskrit epics of ancient India. These two books for Hindus are sacred and often used during special prayer services usually performed at home. I have some vivid memories of when my family performed special prayer services at our house. The brothers were all married and had their children. It was a very tight-knit family, and all looked after each other's welfare.

Lack of interest by others in farming slowly led to a decline in farming income to sustain a large family. To maintain the family, my father and my uncle took recourse to borrow. The debt burden increased, and by 1938 they were forced to declare themselves insolvent, and the mortgagee sold thirty acres of cane land and their houses. This tragic event occurred for several reasons. At a minimum, it was primarily due to the family's lack of interest in farming. This sad event of losing the family's home and the three blocks of land, about thirty acres of freehold land, was unbearable, especially for the women in the family. Women provided the primary support to raise the children, cook, and keep the whole house in order. Also, from my observation, they provide the leadership necessary for the family to make progress in life, as exemplified by my mother, Changi.

The person responsible for this tragic incident was none other than a close member of the family. A freehold land is very precious and one needs to make every effort to keep it. The native Fijian owns up to eighty percent of the land in Fiji. Freehold land is special even to this day. Only a little freehold land is still available in Fiji. So, it is easy to see why the value of freehold land is so much in demand. The children were young and could not fathom the gravity of the situation. However, one thing was clear: Life had to go on.

My maternal grandfather was in India in 1936, and my Nani (my grandmother Sitaliee from Allahabad) had some leeway in assisting their oldest daughter, my Mother Changi. It was a welcome relief. My Nani was a generous woman. She loved her children and would not allow her eldest daughter to have no place to live. Bechu Prasad, my mother's oldest brother, was also anxious to bring my mother relief from her difficulties. Lata Singh, the owner of the Nawaka land, was selling his property to go back to India. With the assistance of Uncle Bechu, Nani managed to buy this land and resettle my mother and her extended family. Of course, my Uncle Bechu Prasad benefited from such a venture by getting the best piece of the property. One might say that this transaction satisfied both parties, however. The total cost of the land was 900 pounds sterling, which equals US $1,223.19. Nani paid the whole sum, but my mother and the family were to repay the total amount annually after the cane harvest since this was on credit. Of course, there is no evidence whether the money owed was paid back to Nani or Nana (my grandfather Ram Phal from Siddarthnagar) by my Uncle Bechu Prasad or my Mother Changi.

My Nani was a wise woman. A mother's love always prevails in time of need.

Ram Phal was married in India and had a daughter. We do not know much about his wife and the child. I visited India in

2010 and had the opportunity to meet Shyam Sunder Maurya and his extended family during the visit. My uncle did not want to talk about my Nana's wife and the child. It was a very exhausting trip for me. Besides, the hotel conditions were deplorable in the village. We were welcomed by my family with open arms and they were delighted to see me. From them, I learned that on Ram Phal's disappearance from the town, his wife and her child left the village and went to her father's village, which was the last they heard of them. This situation was not a surprise since those recruited had truly said little or explained about having any family members affected. Ram Phal left India in 1902, leaving with his wife and a child and two brothers in India. They are dead now, but the children are still alive. One of the brother's sons, Shyam Sundar Maurya, is doing well. He and his son Shubas Maurya are busy, and it was possible to gain knowledge of their family saga.

When Ram Phal arrived in Fiji, he faced fewer challenges than his predecessors. When the Indian laborers came to Fiji under the indentured system, it was more like slavery, like the African people in America. Oppression was common. All worked as laborers in one form or another. Many, if not all, worked under some very harsh conditions. All had to work from sunset to sundown. Survival depended on completing the assigned task for the day. The laborers faced some severe challenges, such as food supply. All received one week's food supply, and there was no more for them if they ran out. Indeed, food rationing was another means of managing people. All situations needed tight control. The living quarters were tiny and they did everything in one room. It was common to find people going hungry daily. There is evidence that their masters beat some, and in some cases, their masters abused women. Conditions were so bad that suicide within the Indian community was a daily occurrence. The task assigned to everyone was such that it was challenging to complete within a day, which meant that earnings were low. I am not sure about the conditions of my family's health issues and concerns, but it is abundantly clear that no one was immune from the harsh treatment of indentured people.

Chapter 5

MY MATERNAL GRANDFATHER'S VILLAGE *in* INDIA

INDIAN INDENTURED LABOR in Fiji is strongly associated with the sugarcane industry. However, it is also true that there was a need for banana, coconut, tea, rubber, and tobacco plantations. With these industries, a good batch of recruits of Indian workers needed assembling. This situation opened the opportunity for recruiters in India. Thus, those who wanted to recruit were required to get a license from the immigration department. At the same time, these recruiters began to create sub-depots for recruitment. In his book *Fiji Indian Migrants*, Gillian states: "The sub-agents were seldom men of high repute. Indeed, they were often ignorant and evil, and some even assumed two names to recruit for Suriname at the same time."[1] They were often shopkeepers and were a cosmopolitan lot[2]. It is also clear that these men belonged to minority communities; they were Jews, Armenians, Indian Christians, Eurasians, and occasionally Europeans. These people were primarily interested in making a quick buck. Making money was their chief motive. The two of the most prominent pastors,

Reverend Andrews, and Reverend Pearson, have concluded that the recruiting agents deceived up to eighty percent of all emigrants[3]. It is also true that women got paid at a higher rate than men. The rates for men were 45 rupees and for women were 55 rupees. The Arkati were also recruiting immigrants for Fiji; however, the Arkatis engaged illegally. They were associated with the recruiters, and without the Arkatis' assistance recruiting would have been extremely difficult. The success of the Arkati was simply the result of being from the same district where recruitment was taking place. It is worth noting that without the support of the Arkati and the recruiters, the indenture system would not have worked.

When visiting India, it became clear who to go after and how the locals got recruited. The recruiters targeted people from Uttar Pradesh. That was because this is one of the poorest states in India and a prime location to entice people to go to other countries with the hope of getting rich. Undoubtedly, the British were very clever in designing the program to be the most effective recruitment system. The reason becomes more apparent when one visits some of the villages of our ancestors. The living conditions are deplorable, and most of the village people are farmers. The villagers are very hard working, and their family ties are solid. Thus, it is hard to believe that anyone wanted to depart from the family unless there was money to be made by temporarily leaving the comfort of home. The Arkatis deceived my maternal grandfather into leaving his village. His family, including his wife and child, did not know nor had any knowledge of him leaving India. The recruiters were not interested in getting the whole family, only young and healthy people. While visiting India in February of 2010, I saw first-hand the conditions of my maternal grandfather's family and their homes. The conditions that caused these people to leave have not changed very much. The atmosphere and the surroundings reminded me of our village in Nawaka.

Specifically, the compound around the home is dusty and dirty based on western standards. Most families keep buffaloes and bullocks at home. It is for their safety and protection. Their income from the farm is inadequate to support the family. The young often leave the village to find work in cities like Mumbai (Bombay) and Kolkata or go to Punjab and Gujarat and work as farm laborers for a pittance. There will be a slight improvement in their lives without proper support from the outside world. For example, most family cooking relies upon a handcrafted material called chula. The ladies who do most cooking have to stand for hours on their feet while preparing meals. In some cases, they may be on their knees as well.

While visiting the family, it became clear how much they appreciate us. My uncle and the family welcomed me with open arms. One of my uncle's sons, Shubhash, led the way in making sure that I was made comfortable in every way. Shubhash works for the Indian government. The other son has a small shop in Naugher, five miles away from the village. Compared to other people around them, their living conditions are much better. It is because my maternal grandfather helped pay for the construction of the building. The family surprisingly had made much progress in the education of their children. Three boys were away in cities studying at different universities. One was studying bachelor's of commerce, which he completed and did his master's of commerce as well. Another was studying pharmacy and was in his second year. Another son was planning to enter engineering college. There is an awakening in the village that only through education can they improve their standard of living and have a better life. India is developing fast, economically and technologically. The villages, in many cases, relate to a tar-sealed road; electricity and freshwater are now available. The fruits of economic development are now reaching most of the villages. The people look to the future with considerable expectations. We do not have any information about our paternal grandfather's village in India. While many of our family members have had the opportunity to visit our maternal grandfather's home, no one has seen our paternal grandfather's house in Gorakhpur, India.

Chapter 6

THE RECRUITMENT SYSTEM *in* INDIA

THERE IS TRULY little debate about the methods used to select Indians to come to Fiji. The British Raj ruled India from 1858 to 1947. This is also called Crown Rule. They had complete control of India and the people and thus the villages. They were able to select the best workers from those available to them. A much different technique was required to persuade those who showed some interest, as most were deceived and coerced into signing the indenture agreement. There are stories about the Arkati hunting vulnerable people looking for any job that could bring prosperity to their families. Once a potential candidate became known, the Arkati would promise them everything from a good income to a beautiful life in paradise. They would then take them to Kolkata and have them complete the necessary paperwork. The documents were in English, and thus the locals had no idea of the language, nor could they understand what they were signing. Initially, the journey began in Kolkata, India. All the recruits from various districts needed a facility where they could stay in Kolkata. They were kept in small rooms as if they were in jail cells. It was much easier to put them on the ship for their journey to the Fiji Islands while still housed in such conditions. Kolkata was the city where all were to embark for this Promised Land (Fiji). No one was allowed to leave the enclosures. It is important to note that these people were British subjects and were supposed to be treated with some respect, although these poor people had no idea what was happening to them. The recruits were required to sign the document before the first-class magistrate that they were leaving India of their own volition. It was a requirement that each person had proper documentation, which would become their official documentation for life. If the documents were not in the correct order, a person could not enter the ship. These documents are still available in Fiji's archives. Once all paperwork was complete, these people were then allowed to embark on the boat.

Life on the ship was very harsh. It was even more difficult since everyone received the same treatment equally, regardless of caste or gender. Many went hungry because food needed rationing. Many could not bear the terrible conditions and committed suicide—the guards threw dead bodies in the sea without regard for the religious requirements of proper corpse disposal. Hindus believe in being cremated, and this was not to be on the ships.

PART II:

THE JOURNEY *and the* LIFE ON THE SHIP

Chapter 7

NEW ARRIVALS *and* SETTLEMENTS IN FIJI

THOSE WHO MADE the trip safely on the ship from Kolkata to Fiji were the lucky ones. The journey was difficult, but they were happy to arrive at their destination finally. Now came the assignment of the location where they would settle. My paternal grandfather, Shiughan, was from Bihar State in eastern India, bordering Nepal. Patna is the state capital. Between 1879 and 1920, eighty-seven coolie ships made voyages, carrying indentured laborers to Fiji[1]. Initially, the vessel brought laborers from Kolkata. But from 1903, all ships brought laborers from Madras and Mumbai. The Indian indenture ships to Fiji took seventy-three days, while steamers took thirty days. It is not clear which ship brought my Aja to Fiji. But he arrived in Fiji in 1895. Our Aji was from Gorakhpur of Uttar Pradesh state, still one of the most backward states in India. They were married in Ba, Fiji. They both came to Fiji under the indentured system. The contract was for five years, and after completing their indenture period, they settled in Ba. They decided on Rarawai, Ba, to be exact.

My maternal grandfather, Ram Phal, was from Siddharthnagar in the state of Uttar Pradesh. He arrived in Fiji in 1902. Our grandmother Sitalee came from Allahabad, also from Uttar Pradesh. She came to Fiji in 1900 on a vessel named *Arno*. Lautoka is where she served her Girmit. My Nana Ram Phal came to Fiji in 1902 and completed his Girmit in Nawaka. He married his wife while in Fiji. Since my grandfather lived in Nawaka and my grandma lived in Lautoka, how did these two people meet, especially since Lautoka and Nawaka are far?

As free settlers, after completing their contract period of five years, they decided to settle at Nawaka, Nadi as cane farmers. Although their land was not very productive, they toiled night and day, and their economic position improved slowly. Later, they moved to the Nadi town area, with far more extensive and better land to grow sugarcane and start dairy farming. Here they also grew vegetables of all varieties for their use and sold them at the farmer's market. Both dairy farming and vegetables provided them with additional cash as the family began to grow.

Chapter 8

THE INDIAN COMMUNITY *in* FIJI

IT IS HARD to understand the lives of the indentured laborers upon their arrival in Fiji. It is primarily because of the way the recruitment system worked. Recruitment was indiscriminate. The Arkati were selected by the British to recruit those who were vulnerable and especially poor in communities from Uttar Pradesh, Bihar, and later people from South India as well. The villagers were unwilling to leave their families, and the Arkati had to venture outside the towns. The Arkati used many devious means to recruit them. They got in people indiscriminately without caste or any other consideration so long as they appeared young and healthy.

Once in Fiji, they housed the laborers in the same barracks regardless of their status in life. For many, this was intolerable. The culture and traditions that the village people were used to in India were no longer possible. All had to use the same toilets, sleep in "lines," and work together in the cane field, no matter their caste in India. Those in the higher caste who were not working in the areas outside suffered most physically and mentally and had no choice with whom they associated. So right from the beginning, it was either you socialize with others or go alone. Going alone may have been all right for a while, but it was not possible to sustain. All those in the group had to mix and socialize with others irrespective of their caste. Our Indian community in a few years was to melt into the casteless community. Besides this, except for religious differences, no other difference existed between Hindus and Muslims. There was a true bond of brotherhood among them. Each one helped the other in times of difficulty and equally shared good times. Indeed, that was the time when indentured laborers and their children actively worked together as one to improve their economic position and live in a new country as one. It was out of necessity to survive in this new cruel world.

Chapter 9

THE SHIUGAHAN FAMILY

SHIUGAHAN, MY AJA, was married in Fiji. Our indentured laborers came to Fiji from Bihar and Uttar Pradesh from around this part of India. My Aja was from Basti, while Aji was from Uttar Pradesh. Her village was in the Gorakhpur district. The Arkati found her while she and a few of her friends were bathing in the river. The Arkati persuaded her to sign the document, not knowing its content or its significance. My Aja came to Fiji in 1895. Around this time, the situation in Fiji had improved due to the efforts made by Indian leaders. Mahatma Gandhi, C. F. Andrews, and other Indian leaders were instrumental in improving the lives of the indentured during this period in Fiji. Both Aja and Aji settled in Votualevu. Life was much more difficult for them because all around them were jungles as well as large trees. They were clearing this, which required demanding work and appropriate tools, which they did not have. We were not aware that many families were around them, but one thing was clear: Life in this new country was challenging, which many did not anticipate nor expect.

Chapter 10

THE RAM PHAL FAMILY

MY MATERNAL GRANDPARENTS were married in Fiji. My grandfather was fortunate to find a female companion as the men outnumbered women. We do not know much about my grandmother. My grandmother was from Allahabad, India. As for my grandfather, some significant facts are available. As previously mentioned, he was married in India and had a daughter from this first marriage. While visiting India in 2010, I tried to get information about this but was unsuccessful. My uncle, who lives in the village, Patni Jungle, Siddharthnagar, Uttar Pradesh, stated that it was no use talking about the past. He was direct and forceful about his feelings, so I dropped the subject. Upon returning from India, I asked my brother about my grandfather's status before he departed from India to Fiji.

He said that the story about his grandfather having a previous child is true. Furthermore, Nana Ram Phal was adamant about not discussing his past among family members for some reason. Both he and his wife were a very dynamic and enterprising couple. Their life began in Nawaka. My mother, Changi, was born in Nawaka Village. A few of his other children were born here as well. He was happy there and wanted to leave behind something that the future generation would remember. My grandfather decided to donate a piece of land and build a Hindu temple for the community. The temple at Nawaka Village continues to perform prayer services and other religious functions. Hindus in Nawaka are appreciative of this small gift from my maternal grandfather.

Later, when their economic position improved, the family moved to Nadi Town. Besides doing cane farming on improved land, they diversified into dairy farming and vegetables for the local market. Trying different methods proved good for raising a family and providing the opportunity to make extra money. It is well known that farming requires more than a few hands; therefore, having a more prominent family is advantageous. At that time, birth control was unheard of, so my Nana and Nani were fortunate in having a large family. They had three boys (Bechu Prasad, Harry Prasad, and Ram Prasad) and four girls (Changi, Ram Raji, Sukh Raji, and Lakh Raji). The oldest child was Changi, my mother. I have been intrigued by my mother's name and asked Brother Jai how my mother was named. My Brother Jai, tells me that my mother was born with five usual fingers and had an appendage attached to her pinky, giving her six fingers. The name "Changi" suggests a person having six fingers. Many Indians believe that anyone with such a trait is fortunate.

PART III:

MY MOTHER CHANGI

Chapter 11

CHANGI'S MARRIAGE

AT THE AGE of thirteen, my mother, Changi, was married to Baijnath, the oldest son of Aja Shiugahan. Baijnath was a very prominent man in his village. The village people highly respected him for his deep knowledge of religious books, particularly the *Ramayana* and the *Mahabharat.* These are two of the books that Hindus hold dearly and often use in their prayers. Undoubtedly, anyone with such knowledge of Hinduism, especially if they could read or write and recite holy books, indeed would be regarded highly in the village. He was often called to settle disputes among the town and the settlement. Also they considered the demeanor and the status of the family to be especially important. I assume my Nana must have made every effort to find a good man for his eldest daughter, Changi. Typically, the elders within the family are called to make the wedding arrangements. Travel from Nawaka to Votualevu is quite a distance. It took hours to travel, especially in the old days. We used horses as the only fastest means of traveling. Ladies, of course, had to walk long distances for lack of a proper transportation system. I only can imagine the wedding party going such a long distance. The Indian wedding party usually lasts for three days on both sides of the family. It raises questions, especially about the cost and who will pay for the wedding ceremonies. Not only is it costly to marry, but also the man must prepare to travel to the bride's home with his party for the marriage ceremony.

One well-known thing is that those who arrived in Fiji during the indenture system had a tough time finding women to marry. It was due to a lack of women during the indenture system. I understand that for every one hundred men, there were thirty-three available women. Sanadhya did not hold back at this inequality and stated that this was legalized prostitution[1].

For the second generation, it was not so challenging. Both Jai Karan (my father) and Bal Karan (my uncle) were married and lived in Votualevu's family unit. The place had rich soil and an excellent opportunity to progress in life. What was needed was hard work and dedication to be productive in cultivating the land. Also, leadership was needed to get things going in the right direction. It also became apparent that Baijnath's death left a big void in leadership that was required. However, it is not clear if all the necessary implements besides the animals needed for farming were available.

Chapter 12

CHANGI'S LIFE *with* BAIJNATH

MOTHER CHANGI WAS married from Nawaka at the age of thirteen. She was the first of Nana Ram Phal's children to be married from her family. One can only imagine all the intricacies of Indian marriages. Not only are Indian weddings highly elaborate, but very costly as well. It must have been quite a challenge for my grandfather to meet all the four daughters' marriage expenses and pay a dowry to the bridegroom's family. The dowry might include money, elaborate gifts such as animals, gold pieces of jewelry, and more. The bride had little to say about what would be reasonable for the groom's side of the family to provide these items. In Fiji, the bride's family had to pay large sums of money to men to marry their daughters. It is the main reason the family preferred to have sons rather than daughters. It is good to know that dowry in marriage is becoming outdated, especially among the younger generation.

Although the bride's side of the family indeed experienced challenges, it was also confirmed that the groom's side did as well, such as traveling a long distance for the wedding ceremony. The wedding ceremony always takes place at the bride's home.

My mother was young when she was married to Baijnath. It was common for Indian parents to get young girls married at a noticeably early age. Girls, in some cases, got married as young as age twelve. There are several reasons for this. One reason that I believe is that the Indian elders feel that, left on their own, girls might do something that could bring shame to their families. Thus, they felt the sooner they were married, the better. Since my grandfather had four daughters to marry, he wanted to meet this heavy responsibility quickly. However, the custom of marrying girls at a youthful age is a thing of the past.

Mother Changi's life with Baijnath was delightful, and the family lived comfortably with two brothers and their families supporting each other. Mother Changi's first child was born within the first year of their marriage. Deo Narayan was the first child, then Jai Narayan, Shiu Narayan, Chandra Kumari, and Shiu Kumar. I feel truly blessed for their support while growing up. It is because of Brother Deo Narayan our family was able to survive some challenging times. I will elaborate on his support of me during most of my teenage years.

Chapter 13

THE DEATH *of* BAIJNATH

MY BROTHER JAI Narayan best describes his father's death. He began by saying that his father had a premonition of his death. Baijnath called all his close relatives and sat in the middle of his big Bure house with a pillow tucked to his stomach. He started by saying how much he loved everyone and wished all happiness and prosperity. He said that he would be dying soon and that they needed to accept this reality. It became apparent the pain and suffering the family would have to endure.

One can imagine the reaction of those present to such words by a dying person. My Brother Jai Narayan described it as unbelievable to everyone present. He says that Baijnath told Jai Karan, my father, to look after his wife and children. The children were Deo Narayan, Jai Narayan, Shiu Narayan, Chandra Kumari, and Shiu Kumar. He passed away just as he had predicted shortly after meeting with his family. It was in the year 1933. After his death, the family observed the traditional thirteen-day ritual. The first step is to collect the ashes of the deceased the next morning. A priest performs the prayer service before all remains plus ashes are placed gently in the water. A Hindu priest performs specific prayer services daily because Hindus believe that the deceased's soul remains around the neighborhood. On the last day, which is on the thirteenth day, the priest performs the prayer. According to the Hindu belief, the deceased's soul will reincarnate.

Chapter 14

MY MATERNAL GRANDFATHER RETURNS *to* INDIA

MY BROTHER TELLS me that my Nana was married in India and had a daughter there. He returned to India in 1936 to his village, but as far as we know he did not make much effort to locate his family. It was because of the method used to recruit the village people. The recruitment system did not allow any time for those affected to say goodbye to their loved ones. Like many, the recruiter deceived him as well. Once in the housing unit, all were locked in and unable to get out from the team. All those brought into this unique building had little to no recourse. Thus, now ready to sail to the Fiji Islands. It raises some pertinent questions as to why he made no effort to locate his wife and daughter. There is truly little information, and many who left India as indentured servants faced a similar dilemma. Since he had his wife in Fiji and all his children, it seems that the decision to search for the lost family may have been on his mind, but given the time frame, it would have been futile.

My mother was born in Nawaka, Nadi. She was married from this village as well. I find it remarkably interesting that I was born in Nawaka, the place of my mother's birth. And here I am, the only child of my Mother, Changi educated enough who is left to tell the family story. All my mother's children were born in Votualevu. It was a challenge to travel during those days due to the distance between the two villages. In the Hindu culture, once a girl gets married, she moves with the husband's family and becomes one of the family members for life. Here is where my Mother Changi faced many challenges in her life. It is also of some significance that my mother's last day of her life was in Nawaka, Nadi. I was able to be with the family in Nawaka Village during her funeral services. From what I heard, she had difficult days before her last breath at the hospital. Hearing this situation, I felt sad that I was not there when she needed me the most. The healthcare delivery system in Fiji is poor compared to Australia, New Zealand, etc. It is also true that many of the Fiji Indians cannot communicate appropriately with the doctors and caregivers. Thus, patients' health is compromised. I, being in healthcare for over forty years here in the USA, would have provided some support that my mother needed at the time.

PART IV:

SHIUGAHAN FAMILY CHALLENGES

Chapter 15

MOTHER CHANGI, NOW A WIDOW

LIFE WAS NOT the same for the family after the death of Baijnath. It wasn't straightforward since he was the head of the family. My Mother Changi was in a challenging situation, and she especially had to raise her own five children. The ages of her children were as follows: Deo Narayan was eight years old, followed by Jai Narayan aged six, Shiu Narayan was five years old, Chandra Kumari was three, and Shiu Kumar was only four months old. Mother Changi needed support from her side of the family, who lived in Nadi Town. My maternal grandparents wanted to take Changi and her family with them to Nadi Town. But this was not agreeable to my mother. Of course, my Nana and Nani were not pleased with my mother's decision. Unfortunately, my maternal grandparents were very unhappy with my mother and stopped visiting her home in Votualevu. As the months elapsed, there was no communication with the family from Nadi. It took my uncle, Harry Prasad, to finally be able to establish contact with my mother.

It was 1936 when my maternal grandfather was away in India. This event was a fortunate one for my mother. It is because Nani (my grandmother) could make independent decisions about how to help her eldest daughter. Nani was able to find 900 pounds of British currency to help purchase the land in Nawaka with the help of Bechu Prasad, my mother's younger brother. It is important to note that the Nawaka property may have provided the opportunity for all of us to achieve our goals in life, including mine, as will be elaborated on later.

My brother Ravindra Nath was born in Votualevu in 1934. Utra, my sister, was born on January 16, 1937. Jai Karan, my father, followed the instructions given to him by his dying brother, and he began to spend more time with my Mother Changi. Jai Karan was already married and had his children, but now he had the responsibility of raising the children of his older brother too. Jai Karan's children were small. It was challenging for Jai Karan to feed and clothe all the children, his and his brother's. The first child was a girl named Suruj Kumari, the second child was a son named Hari Narayan, and the third was a girl named Kamla Wati. The fourth was a girl named Veera Mati. The fifth was a son named Prem Narayan.

During 1937, the burden of raising two families was cumbersome. At the age of twelve, Deo Narayan, Baijnath's eldest, started to work at a store in Nadi. Brothers Deo Narayan and Jai Narayan were both sent to my Nana Ram Phal's home. It was here where my Uncle Harry Prasad was staying as well. It is not entirely clear, but apparently, Brother Deo Narayan returned to my mother's while Jai Narayan remained at Nana's home.

Uncle Harry Prasad was very clever in many ways. He was very fond of his eldest sister, my mother. He knew exactly how to persuade her to send one of her sons and the other sons of my father to help him on his farm. It is not clear whether it was a family decision or a decision made by my mother. It is also unclear whether reducing the number of children at home to lessen the burden of taking care of all the children at home played a role in her decision.

One of the primary reasons for this was that my uncle did not have a son to help him with his large farm and his dairy business, and it was vital for him to get the much-needed help to manage his farm. Among the brothers, Hari Narayan, Prem Narayan, and Ravindra Nath all had spent several years helping him. Jai Narayan stayed the longest, and he gained much from staying at Uncle Harry's home in Nadi Town.

Jai Narayan, who later graduated from Natambua High School, was among the first to complete an education beyond primary school in our family. He later went to Nasinu Teachers' College and qualified as a teacher in 1948. After teaching for hardly a year, he was able to go to India for a university education. It was necessary since Fiji did not have a university during this time. Jai Narayan was a very bright student and was fortunate to get a scholarship to India for his university education. I understand that he left Fiji on a cargo ship named *Sirsa*. Every year, the vessel came to take those to India who had completed ten years of their indenture period in Fiji and wanted to go back to India. It was part of the agreement that they would repatriate to India if they met the ten years in Fiji. Approximately five hundred passengers boarded the ship. Many indentured people wanted to go back after serving their ten years in Fiji. My Brother Jai Narayan had no other choice due to financial constraints but to travel by this ship.

Unlike the luxury liners, the voyage from Fiji to India took a month to reach Kolkata, which would have taken two weeks by luxury liners. He told us that the conditions on the ship were deplorable, and because of the crowding, people had to sleep on the floor. The facilities and the food provided were very unsatisfactory, but his choice in the matter was nonexistent. The desire for a university education was the goal. Thus, any inconvenience was not a consideration.

Once arriving in India, he had to take the train to go to our maternal grandfather's village. I visited India in 2010 and saw first-hand how difficult travel is from Delhi to Siddharthnagar. We took a taxi to visit the family, taking about five days from Delhi, India. It was because we had to take a rest in the evenings at hotels on our way. Imagine Jai Narayan going on a train. The journey was not only tiring, but he faced many hardships along the way.

Chapter 16

CHANGI'S LIFE AFTER *the* DEATH OF HER HUSBAND

AFTER HER HUSBAND'S death, my mother's life changed dramatically. Up till then, she had lived a very protected life confined to home. In the past, women in the Indian community were not self-reliant. They relied heavily on their husbands for everything. In the event of unexpected misfortune, such as the passing away of their husbands, most of them find themselves entirely shattered and helpless. It is common for their parents if they have several children to take some in their care in such situations. My mother found herself in such a situation. Her husband was there to provide for her with whatever she needed. But now, she was made to face life alone.

Sugarcane farming within a village is difficult enough. Still, life is even more challenging without a strong family structure, especially when the eldest son of the Shiugahan family was no longer around. Not only did her five children face a future without their father, they felt isolated within the family unit. Jai Karan, my father, had to provide for his own family and the family of his elder brother, which created a considerable challenge for both sides of the family. Circumstances forced my mother to enter a relationship with my father, Jai Karan. We know that events create the future, and for us to become a judge of right and wrong at this time cannot be justified or be beneficial to anyone. All the first generations of our family are no longer with us, and there is no one around to answer some essential questions that arise for me as I write this book. My father, Jai Karan, had his wife and children; it must have been tremendously stressful for all concerned. Both adults and others must have been confused with what was going on with the Shiugahan family. There is so much unknown, which makes it difficult to find answers to many of the questions. All the Indian families extended or otherwise were protected irrespective of whether the member contributed anything. In the event of some mishap or calamity, all members come together and protect one another.

At the time, no school was close to our home, and living conditions at home were slowly deteriorating. My mother thought her children would be better off if they went to her father's place since they lived in Nadi Town and near by schools. Besides this, she undoubtedly believed that her children at her father's home would be given all the love and care they needed as well. It is unclear whether such a decision to send her kids away to her father's place was prudent, especially since her father was living with his youngest daughter, who had her own children. I understand that my mother's children got poor treatment. My sister Chandra tells me that she had to wake up at three AM to cook for the family of five and to wash all the dishes and clean the house daily. She had to take care of the garden and milk the cows as well. It is common for Indian parents to assist their daughter when she becomes a widow. However, it is not necessarily prudent to do so unless there are no other options. In this case, my mother did not have other options.

My mother's oldest boy, Deo Narayan, was only ten years old, and he was too young to know what was going on. Losing his father at a young age must have been very traumatic and challenging.

Jai Narayan was my mother's second child. He was also very young and could not know of the relationship that began to take place between my mother and my father. My mother decided to send both boys to Uncle Harry Prasad's home. What was the reason for such a separation? Why were they separated from their mother and their birthplace at such a tender age? These questions remain a mystery. One by one, the children of Bajinath were sent away to the maternal side of the family. The two families that were supportive in this regard were my maternal grandparents and one of my uncles. I am also intrigued by what prompted these two relatives to be so willing to accept these youngsters. Was this based on being supportive in their time of need, or was it based on some ulterior motive, such as getting additional hands to help with vegetable gardening and household chores? The latter sounds more plausible, especially since there was an opportunity to generate cash by selling vegetables and cow milk to the local merchants in Nadi Town.

Chandra Kumari, the only daughter of Baijnath, was sent away to her grandparents. Here again, one wonders about the reason for such separation.

Shiu Narayan was also sent away to his grandparents' home. Why? The mystery remains. The only answer might be that Jai Karan did not want to be around children born of my mother's first marriage. It is not the case, I am confident, but who knows the reality of the situation? It is a curious coincidence that all the children needed to relocate from their birthplace. Shiu Kumar was the only child who remained with my mother because he was still young and required his mother's care.

Chapter 17

SHIUGAHAN FAMILY BREAKUP

THE SHIUGAHAN FAMILY was not the same after the death of Baijnath, my mother's husband. Here we see the role of having an older son who is specially dedicated and committed to supporting the family. With such a huge leadership void, the family unit began to deteriorate. It is complicated to imagine how such a close-knit family manages when there is only one person, my father, Jai Karan, who had to bear the burden of the whole family. It was particularly challenging since now, in addition to his own family with children, he had to begin to look after his brother's wife and their kids. My father, Jai Karan, began to spend more time with my Mother Changi, and soon their relationship became more affectionate. Such an arrangement was acceptable within the Indian community: that the younger brother takes the responsibility of looking after his wife and kids on the elder brother's death. It is realistic to assume that Bal Karan, my uncle, and younger brother to Jai Karan, did not care to be around while the family was in such turmoil. He had his share of issues since now there was a massive void in leadership among the families.

My maternal grandfather, Nana Ram Phal, was also interested in wanting to help Changi. His wishes were that Changi would return to live with him. He was determined to provide the support needed to raise his grandkids, but my mother refused to comply. It was because, after marriage, a woman leaves her parents' home, never to go back and live with them again. Thus, she was determined to remain at her husband's home till her death. Her decision to stay back at her husband's house was not taken well by her parents, and they severed their relationship with her and her children. After her husband's death and with five kids to raise on her own, this additional burden must have been challenging. One can only imagine the family troubles multiplying. At the same time, the daily task of household difficulties plus cultivating the land must have led to the development of a relationship between my father, Jai Karan, and my mother.

It was not long before my Brother Ravindra Nath was born while the family was still in Votualevu. Utra Kumari, my sister, was also born in Votualevu. All this was happening while my father had his children from his legal Indian marriage. The family had to accept such events, but such things were common on the other hand. Our Indian community in Fiji was brought from India and made life better for all in the small villages. They faced many difficulties, including negotiating family relationships, stark economic conditions, and medical health issues—all compounded by raising the young ones. The burden of staying together as a family unit was tremendously stressful. It was tough to manage family finances. It is for economic reasons that the joint family slowly disintegrated.

Chapter 18:

AUCTION OF THE FAMILY HOME *in* VOTUALEVU

THE TWO BROTHERS left to manage the farm were somehow did not do a good job; thus, the only option was to auction the Votualevu property. It may also have been a lack of knowledge in keeping good records for monies owed to shopkeepers. I have first-hand experience of this to be the case when we go shopping. There is almost one hundred percent reliance on the shopkeeper who keeps the record of purchases. Those who make a purchase have no way to question whether the amount of money owed is legitimate. According to Sharma, shopkeepers ripped off their clients by charging double the cost. If the buyer paid one shilling, the shopkeeper would write two shillings[1].

My mother was fortunate that my Nani came to her rescue. My Nani was very distressed for my mother and her five children and offered to help the family. Lalta Sing, an acquaintance of Nani's, was selling his property and going back to India. In 1936 Nana was away in India to see his family. He had decided to stay there until the end of 1936. My mother's elder brother, Uncle Bechu, heard that Nani wanted to buy the land to move to Nawaka with her family. With his assistance, Nani purchased the land for 900 pounds. This decision to buy the land would not have been possible if Nana had stayed back. He would not have allowed such an investment, especially since my mother did not obey his request to move back to his home.

The Nawaka land had two parts. Probably the better part went to Uncle Bechu, and the other part, in which Lalta Singh had his house, became our home in Nawaka.

The Jai Karan family also moved to Nawaka and began a new life along with my mother. During this period of uncertainty, Bal Karan, my father's younger brother, had moved to his in-laws' home in Vitongo, near Lautoka. It was difficult for the family, and those affected had to find ways to be with their loved ones and raise their families. It became apparent that this temporary solution did not work out well for him, either, and he had to move back with his elder brother Jai Karan, my father, to Nawaka Village. The Nawaka land that belonged to my Mother Changi was large enough to accommodate the other family members. As I recall, a pundit (a Hindu priest) family was allowed to stay next to our home on a small hill at no cost. It is because my mother and the family believed in providing support to those in need, but more importantly, since he was a priest, we had to provide support in any way we could.

Most of the land in Nawaka was agricultural. We planted sugarcane and rice and had a vegetable garden on the riverbank on the land belonging to native Fijians, who had given the land to us on payment of a little rental house. My uncle, Bal Karan, acquired part of the land across the gravel road. My mother was always very generous in this regard. One of my mother's younger sisters also shared a piece of the land to build her house. While growing up at Nawaka, we never had a shortage of companions. Though we were poor, I have a delightful memory of my childhood days. Our needs were limited, and life was full of fun and joy. It was an excellent environment for us to be around family members, who were our closest friends. As for me being the youngest of my mother's children, I always felt protected by my elders, especially my brothers and my cousins. In this regard, I was able to get away with things that others could not. This type of environment gave me lots of confidence and proved beneficial in my adult life.

PART V:

MOTHER CHANGI'S CHILDREN

Chapter 19

DEO NARAYAN, FIRST SON *of* CHANGI

MY MOTHER'S FIRST child was Deo Narayan. Among Indian families, it is always a great joy when the first child is a boy. The first child being a boy meant a lot to the Shiugahan family. Deo Narayan was a natural gift to our family in many ways. When he turned nine years of age, he began to help and support the family. The family faced a few tough challenges, and Brother Deo Narayan by all accounts saved the family from a disaster. My maternal grandfather was instrumental in Deo Narayan getting married. I understand because of the promise made by my maternal grandfather. Deo Narayan had no choice but to marry the young lady to honor his grandfather's guarantee. It was common among the elders to make such promises, and the new lifetime partners have truly little say.

I have a vague memory of the wedding ceremony. The family of the bride lived quite far from our Nawaka Village. It was common to rent a bus in which those wanting to attend the wedding would ride while the groom would ride in a taxi. Before getting to the bride's home, the groom would get on a horse, and the rest of the guests would follow him in the procession. It is widespread practice to have an Indian priest with the bride's father to greet the groom and his side of the family. After all the formalities, it is the responsibility of the priest to perform the marriage rituals. These rituals are significant; they are routine in all Hindu weddings. The bride's side of the family welcomes the groom and his guests to their home compound. The priest would perform the wedding ceremony. It was a simple wedding. The next day the newlyweds, along with family and friends, would return home, and the family welcomed the bride to her new home. I do remember this part of the marriage ceremony.

Brother Deo Narayan was a person full of love and compassion. He made sure that others' needs came first. Since he did not have any children, it made things easier for him to shower his love and affection on all the other children in the family. All of us who have succeeded in academia owe much to Deo Narayan. It is because of his support I have been successful in my life.

I returned to Fiji after ten years of being in the United States after completing my undergraduate studies. By then, I had a daughter, Beverly, six years old. For our comfort Brother Deo Narayan had built a separate toilet and shower room attached to his house. I have lovely memories of what he did for all of us. These were expensive undertakings, but he incurred these expenses to make us feel comfortable.

We arrived in the evening, and a vast crowd came to the airport to greet us. Everyone looked quite different, but I was able to recognize most of my family members. It was great to see my mother, father, and my uncles, along with sisters, brothers, and a few local village people. What a joy it was to ride back to the village with them. I must admit it was bizarre to see very narrow roads and small buildings along the way. When we arrived at my place of birth, many people from Fijian villages came to welcome us. My wife and daughter both were exhausted and needed rest. We had a particular room designated for us to sleep. Things looked small and crowded; the room was comfortable, nonetheless. We could not sleep much due to the noise level outside. Besides dogs barking continuously, a strong wind was blowing.

The following day we woke up without much sleep and wanted to find ways to tell my mother about our difficulties. After talking with Brother Deo Narayan and my mom, we moved to Brother Prem's home, 66 yards away upon a hill. Prem Narayan lived with my father and his family, so it was acceptable to stay there. Prem Narayan had a new home with an additional room, which was much more comfortable. I understand my Brother Ravindra was instrumental in helping to purchase this modern-day home from a Fijian man who just happened to be the chief of a local village.

Brother Deo Narayan had retired from Samji in Nadi Town. He now had his shop at Nawaka Village; he seemed happier now, and it was great to see him in this situation. It is important to note that he had adopted my Brother Hari Narayan's son. Ajeet was only a few months old when he was adopted. Since Brother Deo Narayan did not have any children, adopting a child from a family member was beneficial for both parties. Ajeet Narayan provided much-needed help in running the shop and managing the land he had leased from Frank Wodhingham, an Australian farmer who had settled in Fiji and owned large pieces of freehold land.

I visited Fiji a few times later and always stayed with Deo Narayan. I always felt pleasure going back to Fiji and made sure that I stayed at Mom and Brother Deo's home in Nawaka.

Chapter 20

JAI NARAYAN, CHANGI'S SECOND SON

LIFE IN VUTUALEVU for Jai and Deo was in some ways great since they had elderly folks around them. One of them was Rauti, who had given a sewing machine to my Mother Changi, which she regarded as one of her most prized possessions. My mother used this machine to make clothes for the family.

Buli Aja was another regular visitor at home in Votualevu. He was Shiugahan's real brother-in-law in India. Both did not know that the other was to go to Fiji as indentured laborers. They were pleasantly surprised to meet each other accidentally in Fiji. Buli Aja had no children, and he showered all his love on our family. When he passed away, his wife came to live with our family at Nawaka.

Changi's second child, Jai Narayan, also played a very significant role in our family. As a young boy, he and Brother Deo were sent away to our maternal grandfather's home. One of the reasons was that the school was close to Nana's home. Besides this, it is also true that my mother could not support her large family after the death of her husband. Brother Jai tells me some stories of having a tough life at Nana's home. He tells me that our Nana was a wise farmer, and he did everything possible to improve his economic position. My brother Jai Narayan had to work extremely hard while under Nana's care. Starting at an early age, he had to get up at three AM and milk cows and distribute milk in the town, and on return from school, he worked on the farm till sunset. He was another farmhand except that he was his grandson.

After milking the cows, the milk needed to be delivered to clients in Nadi Town. Upon his return from this chore, he had to water the vegetable garden. Finally, he would dress up to go to school. The school was in Votualevu, approximately ten miles from Nadi. It must have required a real commitment to travel this distance on foot. I cannot imagine anyone determined to succeed in life as much as Jai was. His graduation from grammar school meant that he had accomplished something no one in our family had. Upon completion of school, he came home to work on the farm once again. All this was routine from Monday to Friday. On the weekends, most of his efforts were toward looking after the sugarcane farming and the cattle.

My mother's two eldest children were the first to come under Nana's care. Deo Narayan, our eldest brother, however, returned home after a short stay. Jai Narayan stayed on, with Uncle Harry Prasad, till 1949. Uncle Harry had a large farm, which he could not manage alone. My Uncle Harry Prasad did not have boys at the time. Thus, he had difficulties managing the sugarcane farm without extra hands. Realizing that the boys could be helpful to him, he convinced my mother to send him boys from Nawaka Village to provide needed help. Despite my father and my elder brother's opposition, my mother continued to send someone to stay at Uncle Harry's home. Besides Jai Narayan, Hari Narayan and Prem Narayan were encouraged to stay at his place and assist on his farm for many years. Ravindra Nath, I believe, also spent some time at Uncle Harry's home, but unlike Hari and Prem, they did not stay at Uncle's for a long time. Changi's insistence on having children from both sides of the family spend some time at Uncle Harrys' home may have been that, in her mind, she was providing them the experience of life in the town rather than being continually in the village. If this was her thinking, we could not know. Or was it her desire to try to help my uncle, who was a knowledgeable man with good intentions?

My Brother Jai tells me that he feels grateful to Uncle Harry and his wife, my Mami, who was always kind and caring. He thinks that were it not for them, he would not be what he is today. Jai Narayan is held in remarkably high regard in Fiji today. He has accomplished much for the people of Fiji. He was the principal of the Indian high school, which is now Jai Narayan College, one of the top high schools in Fiji. Jai was a good student while going to primary school. He used to get exceedingly high marks. His schoolteachers often would relay this to our family. Besides Marist Brothers and Natabua, there were no other high schools in Fiji. Natabua had less than thirty boys (though there were no girls in high school at that time). Jai Narayan tells me that although Uncle Harry had little education, he took an interest in Jai's education and felt happy that his nephew was doing exceptionally well at the school. When he passed the Primary School Certificate Examination at the end of 1942, convinced by Headmaster Shinju Reddy, my uncle decided, with the help of my parents, to send him to an exclusive boarding school at Natabua. Natabua had less than thirty students, and only seventeen were in the boarding facility. The total boarding school fee was approximately ten pounds a year, which was beyond most Indian families to pay at the time. It was not so easy for Uncle Harry and my parents to find such money. He stayed at Natabua in the boarding school for four years, and the family jointly supported him despite facing financial uncertainty. Uncle Harry had several flaws in his character, but he was a kind-hearted and very caring person—a good Samaritan.

Without a doubt, Brother Jai Narayan opened the door for all those who followed his path searching for higher education. He was the first in our family to be able to attend high school.

He recalled the Second World War (1939–1945) when the American army made their base at Nadi to fight the Japanese forces whose occupation had reached the Solomon and Gilbert Islands. Brother Jai remembers Uncle Harry Prasad worked whole nights driving while aerodromes at Nadi's potential construction project were discussed among the elite (now part of Nadi International Airport). My maternal grandfather had leased out a large tract of grazing land from the Fijian landowners, and he used to keep animals, cows, and horses belonging to others for two shillings a month. When the animals saw the airplanes in the air, they were frightened. All over the grazing land, the cows started running and mooing, and the horses were galloping all over the place, making weird sounds. He was frightened and felt doomsday had come.

In the beginning, there was no post exchange for soldiers, and there were thousands and thousands scattered all over the country in "camps." Nadi was then a small town with about ten shops. There was a Chinese shop (Kempo's); the owner started selling fresh lemonade to the soldiers. Lemons and oranges grew wild in the forest, and Jai used to bring sacks full of lemons to the camps, and in return, he used to get two colored candies for the hard work.

There was only one newspaper printed in Fiji in those days, *The Fiji Times*, but Jai says that he never saw one. It reached only the elite class. He remembers only Nadi Town having one radio at Narottam's shop. At that time, only one private doctor was practicing in Nadi, Dr. Mukerjee. He was married to a German woman, and he understood English. In the evening at Narottam's, small groups of people would gather around to hear the world news. Dr. Mukerjee, without fail, would be there. He would tell whatever he heard from the noisy radio and relate the message to his friends present. One such friend was Pundit

Hardyal Sharma. Whatever Pundit Sharma told us was actual news to others, including Jai. There was certain news for Fiji on Saturdays, provided by a government clerk, speaking from Smile's barber shop at eleven-thirty AM for half an hour. During this time, there was limited local news coverage provided to a handful of people. Thus, the privileged few got world news, and the rest were totally in the dark.

Few American soldiers, especially those stationed in the Nadi Town area, seemed happy with their location. At the time, Jai was in form three at Natabua High School. Thus, he was able to speak a little English and was able to understand the American soldiers. Some of the American soldiers loved horses and wanted to ride them. Uncle Harry Prasad provided horses by charging fifty cents an hour. Since Jai spoke English, this venture turned out to be a wonderful experience to learn about the outside world. Jai also was able to tell the American soldiers about the world news, which they were interested in knowing.

In addition to American soldiers having a base in Nadi, they also spread around Nawaka Village areas. The Indian people did not know English, and it was difficult for them to converse with them. But they learned many common swear words from them! While all this was taking place, Jai continued his schooling and was able to pass both the Junior and Senior Cambridge Certifications. Since there was little opportunity to further his education, he decided to go to Fiji's teacher's training school, which he completed without any difficulties. Once he got his credential, he began to teach immediately to make some money plus gain experience. He decided to give all his earnings to Mami, my Uncle Harry's wife. When he was leaving for India, he got ninety-four pounds from Uncle Harry, which was the money that he had earned in a year while teaching at a school in Fiji. It was a welcome gift for expenses while traveling to India on a ship.

Since the school was still closed, Brother Jai Narayan stayed at our grandfather's village for months. While in the town, he experienced first-hand the life of our family. It was not much different from village life in Fiji. He said he was getting used to the village life in India. One night, he and the family saw lots of people on horseback with flashlights. He learned that these were criminal gangs across the border from Nepal, and as they often do during the summertime, they had come to steal things from people in India. He was also alerted that these criminals might harm him since he was a foreigner. On the same night, he left the village and got on the train going to Lucknow.

He was fortunate to get into the Christian college in Lucknow. After a year or so, he enrolled at Lucknow University, where he received his bachelor of arts in education and license in teaching. Brother Jai Narayan was always interested in teaching. In fact, before leaving for India, he went to Nasanu Teaching College in Fiji. It was not a college and was called such because there was no college or university in Fiji. After a year at the teaching college, the student was qualified to teach at a high school level.

While still at the university, he met his future wife, Irene. They were married in India against the wishes of Irene's family. We Indians from Fiji do not fit in the category of being in the high class. They identified us as coolies by Indian standards. It is considered a low caste. In any case, after their marriage, they had to leave Lucknow and go to Banaras University. This university is the largest in India and has a very high standard. Here, Jai received his master's in education. It was a significant hardship for the two of them, especially since they now had a child. Brother Shiu Kumar was also studying at the University of Mumbai (Bombay) for a BS degree in biochemistry. Imagine being united with your brother in this foreign land after several years of being apart. It is also significant to see that the brothers fully embraced each other and tried to support each other.

On their return, both joined D.A.V. College in Suva. Later, Irene Jai Narayan became the principal of D.A.V. Girls College and later joined the late Mr. Gopal Bhai to start the M.G.M. High School in 1965. Mr. A. D. Patel, a leading Indian politician and prominent lawyer, persuaded her to enter politics.. It was in 1966 when she became a member of the legislative council. In 1970 she was part of the Indian delegation that represented the Indian community in Fiji for Fiji's independence from British rule. Irene Jai Narayan retired from politics in 1992.

Chapter 21

SHIU NARAYAN, CHANGI'S THIRD SON

BROTHER SHIU NARAYAN was the third child of my mother. As a young boy, he also was placed in my maternal grandfather's care at the age of eight. Being a very gifted student at an early age, he took great interest in going to school. However, like other of Changi's children, he was unable to continue schooling beyond fourth grade. His grandfather convinced him not to go to school but to work on his dairy farm full time and do gardening and other chores around the farm as needed. My maternal grandfather, for some reason, took a particular interest in him and persuaded him to be around him all the time.

When he grew up, he took an interest in carpentry and joined the building section at the Nadi airport. He reached the position of head of this section after working there for a few years. He could be a great leader at the firm, but lack of adequate education was a factor in remaining at a low-level position. He was well-liked by his fellow workers as well as our village people. I have a few vivid memories of his wedding at home. Nana Ram Phal especially liked Brother Shiu Narayan, so he wanted to know that his marriage would be memorable. He brought in a very well-recognized dance company to perform on the second evening of his wedding at our home in Nawaka Village. In a Hindu marriage, the groom's side has three main parts.

The first evening is called Mehndi night. During this evening, the ladies from the immediate family cover the groom with oil mixed with turmeric. It is a very significant evening for the grooms' mom and sisters. They take turns placing this oil on the groom accompanied by background music. The second night is called bhatwaan. This evening is all about entertainment for the guests. I was only seven years old, but I do have significant memories of the evening. The next day is where the groom's family leaves for the bride's side of the family. Here again, my Nana Ram Phal did not hold back on expenses. As the groom was getting into his car, he took a handful of coins and cast it over the groom's head for all to see. The kids ran and picked up the coin's pennies, which gave us lots of happiness. The groom was then whisked away with his family and was a special guest at the bride's home for the wedding ceremony. Brother Shiu Narayan was a favorite child of my mom and my Nana Ram Phal. So, you might say he was spoiled.

Brother Shiu Narayan passed away at the age of fifty-five. He had three sons and three daughters. One son, Jitendra Narayan, was qualified as an electrical engineer. Jitendra was an exceptionally bright student and received an award for a scholarship to study engineering in Australia. As with several students from Fiji, Jitendra faced some unique challenges in Australia and had to migrate to New Zealand, where he finally completed his studies with remarkably exacting standards.

Upon completing his studies, he returned to Fiji and joined the Fiji Electricity Authority (F.E.A.). He, at the time, was the only one recognized for his excellence in helping Fiji improve the life of many. Brother Shiu Narayan's children (except for Jitendra, who passed away) now live in Edmonton, Canada, and all are doing well.

Chapter 22

CHANDRA KUMARI, CHANGI'S FIRST DAUGHTER

CHANGI'S FOURTH CHILD was a girl. Chandra Kumari, the older daughter, was sent away from her mother's home to spend a few years with her Nani at their home in Nadi Town. Chandra Kumari, at the time, was only seven years old. Here is another example of Changi's difficulties raising her children after her husband passed away. Giving up the only daughter to be raised by your parents must have been very difficult. It had to be particularly painful since Chandra Kumari would be at her auntie's home with her children. She faced some cruelty from her grandmother. She was required to rise early to help with the vegetable garden and the morning chores, including cooking for the family. Nana and Nani stayed with their youngest daughter at the Nadi township. They had a large family to take care of, ranging from ages one to ten. Of course, both Nana and Nani were not interested in Chandra's welfare. Still, they demanded that she perform all household duties, including cooking, washing dishes, and cleaning the house. Our Mausi also was required to perform all tasks in raising her children. Our Nani made sure that the women performed all duties around the home and outside of the house.

When she describes her childhood days, she begins to cry and stops talking about this period in her life. One can only imagine that this girl had to take on the responsibilities of family chores that an adult would have difficulty dealing with at seven years. It is particularly true being in an Indian family. She somehow managed to return home. Likely, my mother must have come to learn about the way she was treated and taken her back home.

Chandra's return home was such a relief. She was finally with her mother and her brothers. But her stay with the family was short-lived. Chandra was married off at the tender age of thirteen to Narayan Datt of Meigunyah Nadi. One of my uncles, a schoolteacher, arranged this marriage. The bride-to-be had no say in the matter. I was only seven years old and remembered this wedding very well. My half-sister Suruj, Karan's first born, was also married on the same night. The family had to have two weddings at the same time because of economic reasons. Indian weddings are costly. The marriage ceremony can last for up to three days, and during this time, every invitee gets vegetarian meals. Up to three hundred guests from local villages, and, of course, all family members get invited to the wedding. By having two weddings at once, the family could save on expenses.

Sister Chandra has five daughters and three sons. All lived happily in Meigunyah, Fiji, for several years. Unfortunately, one of the sons passed away at a very tender age. The girls were all married and lived away from their immediate family. Narayan Datt was a good provider for the family. He worked on his farm and also worked at the Nadi airport. He raised vegetables for the family and had enough to sell at the Nadi market. Sister Chandra had two more children later; the two boys and the family migrated to the USA more than twenty years ago and have settled in the San Francisco Bay Area. As with other family members, I provided the necessary documents to allow them to come to America.

Narayan Datt passed away a year ago. I was in Fiji and, at the time, informed of his passing. I made the necessary arrangements to come back to be with the family during his funeral services. One son also passed away some years ago. Salesh's passing was hard for my sister, and to this day, she has lots of fond memories of him. The rest of the family continues to do well in California. Now the family has increased several-fold. It is good to see all doing well.

Chapter 23

SHIU KUMAR, CHANGI'S FOURTH SON

MY MOTHER'S FIFTH child was named Shiu Kumar. He was only four months old when his father passed away. As mentioned earlier, it is hard to comprehend the difficulty my mother faced during this time. It is challenging when the Hindus must perform the ritual of death, which lasts thirteen days. They perform special prayers for the deceased to guarantee the soul will gain the next life. Changi and the family must have been tough to complete this mandatory service when they had celebrated a son's birth just a few months before.

Shiu Kumar had a normal childhood. At an early age, while growing up in Votualevu, he was oblivious to the turmoil brewing within the family. There was not much information available about him until the family moved to Nawaka Village. To the best of my knowledge, he must have attended the Andrews Government Primary School, a prominent school for our village children to attend. I do remember him being an excellent soccer player.

Most importantly, he was an excellent student and always was top of his class at the elementary school. He was one year ahead of my Brother Ravindra Nath at Sri Vivekananda High School. I did have one very vivid memory of him when he began to work at the Nadi airport after he completed high school. He started working at Nadi Airport, preparing food for airline passengers. He was able to bring grapes home every so often. During those days, this fruit was new to us and was not readily available for us to purchase. For us, this was a real treat but it did not last long, for he was accepted at a university in India to further his education.

After completing four years of high school, he was able to go to India for a university education. While in India, he met up with his brother Jai Narayan and his wife, Irene, in Mumbai for a few weeks. It must have been great for them to get together after not seeing each other for a few years. Both brothers were diligent students and were able to complete university without much trouble. After getting a BSc with honors in biochemistry, he returned to Fiji and worked as a teacher for a year. Shiu Kumar was not happy with teaching in Fiji and decided to further his education. He had met a classmate while studying in India who had gone to Germany to study medicine. Shiu Kumar left Fiji and joined his friend in Germany to study medicine as well. It is interesting that Shiu Kumar did not know the German language and could still become a doctor in Germany.

My mother had to keep Shiu Kumar with her after his father's death. It is unclear why my mother began to become close to Jai Karan after her husband's death. After the death of her husband, my mother had three options: one was to manage on her own with five children. Option two was to go to her father's home (her father wanted her to return home). Option three was to remain with her husband's family. It was not possible for a young Indian woman, a widow, to manage independently during that age and time. To return to her father's home also did not appeal to her. It must have been tough for her to remain at her husband's home or return to her father's house in Nadi. It was customary practice within the Indian community for a widow to stay at her husband's home if the younger brother would accept her as his wife. My father, Jai Karan, was married and had several children to look after. Indeed, it must have been challenging for my mother to decide. Of course, my father, Jai Karan, was honor-bound to obey his elder brother's dying wish. He accepted my mother as his second wife. Jai Karan lived up to his promise. He loved his brother's children more than his own, and they, in turn, loved and respected him for all he did for the family throughout his life.

Six months after Baijnath's death, Shiughan, my paternal grandfather, passed away. The burden of maintaining the affairs lay in the hands of Jai Karan and Bal Karan, who was entirely inexperienced for such work. Shiugahan and Baijnath controlled and managed the farm and looked after the welfare of each member of the extended family. Bal Karan, my uncle, loved music and singing and had no interest in farming. Left mostly alone, Jai Karan could not carry on the heavy burden of providing for the family and maintaining three blocks of Colonial Sugar Refining Company (C.S.R.) land, every ten acres. Jai Karan, my father, continued to provide for the family and kept borrowing money from money lenders. Who were these money lenders, and what was the amount of money owed to them? Indeed, a reasonable question and we will not know the absolute truth.

Nevertheless, the farms needed selling so that they could pay off the debtors. In the end, they all became insolvent, and whatever the family had was sold to pay the mortgage. It was a sad day indeed that everything that the family owned required selling. Unfortunately, at the time, the widespread practice among the farmers was to get needed items, mostly food, on credit from those who had shops and pay them the money they owed after harvesting the sugarcane. As one can see, without productive farming, there was no cash to pay the credit due to the shopkeepers.

Chapter 24

RAVINDRA NATH, CHANGI'S FIFTH SON

RAVINDRA NATH WAS born from my Mother Changi's second relationship, with my father, Jai Karan. He was born in 1934. The family continued to live in Votualevu while having to deal with much turmoil around them. One could just imagine the lives of children growing up when the family faced real tragedy. I am not sure if the children were aware of their surroundings or had enough to eat during this time. Of course, they were dependent on their parents for support. It was not until the family moved to Nawaka Village that life began to change for all, especially when they started elementary school. I have a few vivid memories of Ravindra Nath while growing up in Nawaka Village. Besides being an outstanding soccer player, he also had a talent for other sports. I remember seeing him doing pole jumps as well as playing field hockey. One incident that was interesting and sad was when he had planted watermelon next to his home. The land was for growing rice; thus, the site got filled up with lots of water when it rained. The watermelon plants were doing well, and he had a good crop. One night there was torrential rain. In the morning, all the watermelon was floating above the water. There was no way to save the watermelons, and all were spoiled. It was an unfortunate event and a lesson well learned.

There was a second incident at the elementary school. I remember playing soccer during the lunch break with a few other school kids on the playground. Brother Ravindra handed me this vegetable to eat. He had just returned from the Nadi Town market where he had gotten this vegetable. I had no idea what it was. But I did start to eat the green part, and he began to laugh. "No, no, don't eat that part. Eat the yellow part. It is called a carrot." So, I did eat the carrot and liked it. Brother Ravindra was very protective of me and looked after my welfare. I guess it may have been because of our mother. However, he was aware of making every effort to protect me from getting into any kind of trouble. As I recall, my mother ensured that I was well cared for by all in the family as I was her youngest son and her last child.

Chapter 25

UTRA KUMARI, CHANGI'S SECOND DAUGHTER

MY MOTHER'S SECOND child with my father was a girl named Utra Kumari and she was born in Votualevu on January 16, 1937. Now my mother had five boys and two girls. Here again, the family continued to face challenges due to the inability to maximize farming productivity.

When the family moved to Nawaka Village, there was hope that our family life would improve. My sisters all started to go to Andrews Government School, the only elementary school around us. This school was about three miles from our village, thus it was a challenge to get to during the rainy season. Utra, my sister, was not able to go beyond class three at this school. The reason is not apparent, but my father and the family decided that she should get married. She was fifteen years of age, which was considered old during those days. As well, I understand my half-sister Veera was also getting married at this time. The sisters got married in the year 1953.

Sister Utra's marriage was with Raj Narayan, who at the time was twenty-two years old. Raj Narayan and the family were from Malolo. Though we lived in different villages, I remember going to school with a few of Bechu Prasad's children. After the marriage, Raj Narayan and Utra moved to Mala Mala. It is not clear, but they were not compatible with the in-laws. The eldest man of their home was instrumental in helping them move. He, at the time, had properties in both cities and was remarkably close to Raj Narayan and my sister.

PART VI:

MATERNAL GRANDMOTHER'S HELPING HAND

Chapter 26

THE FAMILY MOVES *to* NAWAKA VILLAGE

I WAS BORN in the Nawaka village on February 19, 1939. I am the eighth child of my Mother, Changi, and the last son of Jai Karan from my mother, Changi. My Nani helped secure this village when my mother and her family's home got auctioned off in Votualevu. My maternal grandmother came to the rescue. She could not bear seeing the pain and suffering of her oldest daughter and her grandchildren any longer. It is unimaginable to think of the impoverished welfare of Changi's children during this uncertain time, especially with her younger children. Thus, moving totally to a new location must have been devastating for the family.

My mother had lived a highly protected life, dependent on her husband for her and her children's needs. Upon her husband's death, she found herself incapable of doing anything on her own. It was a tradition within the Indians that upon the end of an elder brother, his wife and children become the responsibility of the younger brother. My father, Jai Karan, was married and had several his children at the time. One can only imagine what the life of a family became after the death of an elder brother, along with the loss of the property and being alone to deal with developing a new family. My father, Jai Karan, had to keep all family members together now. Indeed, a challenging task, especially since all other family members were not there to provide the moral support as needed.

From all indications, the two wives of Jai Karan lived together in harmony with each other. The family lived as one unit. I remember it well, how we all ate out of food cooked in one kitchen. Each one of us ate at our convenience, thus there was no formal sit-down for dinner.

Family life was simple, and it was not much of a challenge to get along. I still have vivid memories of when there was meat cooked. The only type of meat allowed was chicken, goat, or lamb. Fish and eggs were allowed, but we did not get to eat fish, even though there was fresh water and the sea all around us. I often wonder what the reason could have been for not eating more fish at our home. Could it be due to cash flow? It was always a challenge to feed all the mouths in the family. One of the ways to manage this was that we raised our chicken for meat. The chickens also laid eggs. We would usually butcher one chicken for an evening meal. Since one chicken was not enough to feed all of the family members, it was common for the cooks to add lots of water, thus making it like a soup to eat the chicken curry with rice. Often pieces of meat were hard to get. The chickens raised at home tended not to have much meat. Thus, getting a piece of meat was a luxury. We also raised goats for meat, but this was for special occasions, such as Christmas or special religious ceremonies. We did not raise pigs since we were not allowed to eat pork meat. We often had canned fish curries with potato. I always enjoyed this simple dish and often ate it with roti.

Dhal and rice were always available. It was because we raised our rice; however, we had to purchase dhal from a nearby store. My mother and my kaki (Jai Karan's first wife) and other family members constantly faced the challenge of feeding some twenty mouths. It is curious how the decision got made on the type of food available for the day, such as meat, canned fish, or dhal. Indeed, it was a test of their imagination and ingenuity to get everyone fed. We did not go hungry, and to the best of my recollection, we always had enough to eat, albeit small portions. No one ever complained. Everyone felt satisfied with what they received on their plate.

While growing up in a large family, I felt very secure and protected. The unity of family proved to be advantageous as we all were able to gain respect from other kids around our village. We were free from being bullied by others. My cousin's brother, Vidya Nath, was a fierce and strongly built young man whom the village people admired. He was always very protective of us and assured us not to be afraid of anybody. He stood tall in our village. With him by our side, we had no one to fear. He had a particular liking for me and always called me Babua (a little brother). I will never forget his kindness and unique supportive nature for me.

Chapter 27

MY LIFE AFTER NADI PRIMARY SCHOOL

AFTER COMPLETING CLASS eight education, I began to work on the family farm in Nawaka Village at thirteen years of age. Farming life was complicated and functioned at a very hectic pace. There was always work to do, and it was a family affair. Many people believe that having a large family is good because more hands are available to do the work. It is strictly my opinion that multitasking is necessary in farming.

After completing primary school, up to the eighth grade, those who wanted to go to high school needed to take a test; I took the test and managed to pass the high school entrance test and got accepted to attend the Vivekanand, a prestigious high school in Nadi and the only one around us during that time. It is no coincidence that my two brothers Shiu Kumar and Ravindra Nath completed their high school education there. At the time, the school was next to Nadi Bridge. It is because a small number of students were from local villages. Some teachers were from India, and I understand that the teaching quality was of an extremely high standard.

I remember going to this high school for just a week. In those days, I did not have shoes or the proper uniform to attend school. My Brother Ravindra gave me his pair of sandals, and Brother Deo Narayan arranged a local tailor to make my uniform. After my first week, I had to withdraw from this high school. My older brother Ravindra Nath received an acceptance letter to go to Canterbury University in Christchurch (a city in New Zealand). It meant that I could not continue to go to high school. I am not sure if anyone in the family could have made any difference in arguing in my favor. Frankly, traditionally this had to be. There is a firm belief that the older brothers have priority over the younger ones. Our family was still intact, and we needed two hands to work on the farm full-time. Dad was getting older and could not work as he used to. Besides, a few capable hands were not interested in farming. One of the brothers was at Uncle Harry Prasad's home, helping him with sugarcane, dairy farms, and vegetable gardening.

I had to work on the farm on a full-time basis at the time. Sugarcane farming is hard labor and most challenging, especially on hot days. In Fiji, it was hot every day. I can only imagine what our grandparents had to endure on the farm daily during their indentured days. It must have been not very easy indeed for the simple reason that the Girmitiyas were under stringent guidelines to ensure maximum production. It was not unusual to work the entire day without taking any breaks to complete the task allotted. Although the conditions had changed dramatically, one thing that did not change was the climate. Fiji is a hot country. People who must work in an open environment have to withstand hot weather conditions daily. The temperatures can easily reach up to ninety degrees. Sugarcane farming required hard manual labor and the help of ox and ploughs since heavy machinery was not available to us during that time. It was simply expensive for most farmers. I remember getting up around three AM to prepare for farming.

Since one of the sugarcane properties, about fourteen acres (about half the area of Chicago's Millennium Park) of flat land, was far from our home, it took about an hour to get there. I would start working on the farm by around five AM so that I could stop when the temperature would reach its high, which was at about ten AM It got hotter between ten AM and two PM, and the animals' energy levels, including mine, began to decline. I used to work until ten AM and then quit to feed the animals and take them to the river for a drink of water. I would then let them graze until two PM After the animals were fed and watered, the entire process started again, and I would work until sunset. It was better to do the work in the evening because it was much more relaxed.

The first year on the farm was the most difficult one. It was because there were only two of us, and we had to do everything. Hari Narayan, my brother, and I were always involved in farming. We farmed sugarcane most of the time, but we also planted rice, several types of beans, corn, and garden vegetables for our use. My Brother Hari Narayan was a very decent man and was very patient with me. He was always willing to assist me as needed. Of course, during weekends, we had extra hands to get much of the work done. The most important work was to pull the weeds from growing around the sugarcane and deliver the fertilizer. My Brother Hari Narayan and I would keep the soil as soft as possible between the sugarcane roots. We also needed hands during the planting of rice. Once the rice came to maturity, it required harvesting. The harvesting of rice required all available hands from our family. All hands included women and adult children to harvest rice plants with a scythe.

PART VII:

THE STRUGGLE *of* MY TEENAGE YEARS

Chapter 28

THE STRUGGLE *of* MY CHILDHOOD

SINCE OUR PRIMARY school was about three miles away from our village, some kids attended Andrews Government Primary School. We walked to school every day from our home in Nawaka. Going to school was fun, even though the distance was an issue. We did not have any shoes, so walking barefoot was routine, especially when it rained. It was always a challenge to walk barefoot when the road conditions deteriorated, and we had to walk on the boggy road. Unfortunately, the roads then were not tar-sealed. The roads were under repair regularly.

We felt happy during the months when the mangoes were in season. Returning from school was always fun, for we could pick mangoes from any tree freely on our way back from school. Both sides of the road were lined with mango trees, and there were guava trees also. It was fun growing up in this manner. We always traveled with more than five in a group and felt protected by our numbers. We walked to school with our family members, mostly girls of my age. My younger siblings, the boys, did not travel with me since they were much younger. One of my cousins and I were close and helped each other pass letters to share with our friends. I remember giving her a note to give to a girl that I liked, and in return, she would give me her letter to give to a boy that she liked. There was little going on in relationships that we would keep a major secret between us. While playing soccer, one of the letters that I had written got lost. This very innocent letter somehow got in the hands of her brothers, and the next thing that I heard was that they were going to beat me up. From that day onward, I started thinking of leaving Fiji.

My father registered me as Chandra Prakash in class one. It was not until I finished class eight when my name was Jagjiwan Narayan, a name that was given to me and is on my birth certificate. We needed to find my birth certificate to fill the application form to sit for the entrance examination for secondary school. I was successful in passing the entrance exam for Vivekananda High School, the school in Nadi Town where my two brothers had attended. My brothers Ravindra Nath and Shiu Kumar both were talented students and were good soccer players, and played in the senior district team.

One incident that is very vivid in my mind was over a weekend. All the family members had to lend a hand when we needed to plant sugarcane. It happened to be the weekend when Shiu Kumar and Ravindra Nath had to play soccer. My father insisted that it was vital that they stay on the farm and plant sugarcane with the family, as was the custom. Many students from Vivekananda School came in a taxi and implored my father to let my brothers play soccer. Finally, my dad gave in and let the boys go. I was delighted to find that it was because of my brothers' efforts that the school won the match. Indeed, it was a proud moment for our family.

Chapter 29

HIGH SCHOOL

IT WAS VITAL for me to be able to go to Vivekananda High School. The school was close to our home, and two of my brothers had already attended. Also, other high schools were much further away, and it just did not make any sense to take the entrance exam. So, I sat for the entrance exam for Vivekananda High School. I was pleased that I passed, and I began attending.

The school was on the bank of the Nadi River, close to the bridge that separated a Namaka Fijian village and the Nadi town. It was not a large building, and it did not look like a school but was regarded among the best high schools in Fiji. The school had a uniform code. It required a pair of white short pants and a white shirt for children or a white dress. I needed to have these clothes before attending school. In addition to the clothing requirement, I also needed a pair of shoes to complete the uniform. Brother Ravindra was kind enough to provide me with the necessary items. Luckily, I was able to wear them, and everything went well. I was pleased to attend my first class when the school opened; it was like a dream come true. Our home was about four miles away from school, which meant we had to get up early to begin walking on the gravel road to get to school on time. It was exhilarating to walk through Nadi Town to get to school. Once on the school grounds, it was a moment to behold as all the young boys and a few girls had proper attire and were ready to start class.

We were in form one, and the classes taught the basics. The first morning course was math, then English, Hindi, and geography. It felt great to be sitting with some of the students that I had completed my class eight with in primary school. Some students were new to me. The week I spent in high school was a welcome experience.

Chapter 30

RAVINDRA NATH, NEW ZEALAND BOUND

MY ATTENDANCE AT high school sadly ended within a month. My brother Ravindra received an acceptance letter from Canterbury University in Christchurch, New Zealand. Within a few weeks, he had to be in New Zealand to start at the university. I was oblivious to the drama that was to play out after hearing of this new development. Once made aware, there was no reason for me to stress. Being from an Indian family, it was clear the decision my family would make.

A family dilemma was in the making. What to do now since we had two brothers already studying overseas at universities? Both Jai Narayan and Shiu Kumar were already in India attending their respective schools. Fiji, at this time, did not have a university and anyone wanting to further their studies had to leave the country. Shiu Kumar needed financial assistance while studying in India. When it came to family finances, only our elder brother, Deo Narayan, understood finance. It was primarily because of his employment at a shop in Nadi Town. Not only did he understand finance, but also, he was able to borrow much-needed money from where he was employed. Brother Deo Narayan at the time worked at Samji's store. Mr. Samji and his family had lots of faith and trust in him and did not hesitate to give the money needed as a loan.

Thus, Brother Deo Narayan was able to provide the necessary financial support to Shiu Kumar. During this time, I am not sure if anyone in the family knew how much and how often Brother Shiu needed such financial aid. My Brother Deo Narayan was the only one who knew most of our family's needs. Since he worked at Samji's shop, he would use the company truck to bring groceries to our home every month. He also kept track of the expenses and would pay for household needs. Brother Shiu Narayan also worked at the Nadi airport and contributed to our family as needed. No one in the family knew how much money he earned and his share of financial contribution to the family's resources.

On the other hand, Brother Jai Narayan did not need any support from our home while in India. Uncle Harry Prasad had agreed to provide the help he needed. And if Brother Ravindra Nath were allowed to go to New Zealand, he would need our family to finance his expense. Our family was not wealthy. Cash was hard to come by. Brother Deo Narayan was the only one that could get some money to provide the much-needed support.

Also, it was necessary to consider the need for an extra pair of hands at our family farm in Nawaka. Brother Hari

Narayan was the one son who worked full time at our family farm at home. He needed, at minimum, another person to help with the farm. Brother Hari especially during the sugarcane harvesting time, needed help. This help was hard to come by when the three boys were not around. Brother Shiu Narayan was already working at the airport, while Brother Deo Narayan was at Samji's store. Brother Prem Narayan was at Uncle Harry Prasad's home. If he had returned home and looked after the farm, he would have solved the problem of having additional labor on the farm. Unfortunately, on my mother's insistence, he remained at Uncle Harry's place. In retrospect, looking back, it makes me wonder why my mother would make such a decision. I am confident that she wanted me to attend high school, but the choice must have been challenging to make. My attending high school meant that I might follow the path taken by three of her boys after graduating. Being the youngest of her children, this could be a potential reason for deciding as she did.

Chapter 31

FAMILY DECISION ABOUT MY FUTURE

FINALLY, I DECIDED to stay home to help on the family farm and stop going to high school. Additionally, I had to accept the decision made by my family. Ravindra Nath left for New Zealand since he had to start university upon his arrival. Most of us went to the airport to see him catch the plane for New Zealand. At the time, I was not angry nor upset at anyone and did not know what the future would be like for me being on the farm. I had to accept the decision and move on with my life. It was just that simple for me at the time. I was only thirteen years old and had to rely on my elders to make the best decisions for all concerned. There was little that I could have done at that time anyway. What was most important was that I had to follow the decision of my elders.

PART VIII:

FAMILY FARMING *on a* FULL-TIME BASIS

Chapter 32

SUGARCANE FARMING

IT IS HARD to believe that I was a full-time farmer—a reminder of my grandparents' life when they came to Fiji from India. Of course, there is no comparison for the suffering and humiliation they faced compared to my situation, except that it felt like I had no say in the matter once the family had decided. I began working on our family farm daily. Sugarcane farming is difficult, especially since we had to do everything manually. Rice farming is similar. The significant difference is that rice farming requires muddy soil for good production yield, while sugarcane does not. Both kinds of agriculture required getting up around three AM. Depending on the day's activity, in the case of sugarcane farming, I used to get the oxen ready with appropriate tools and travel for over an hour to reach the sugarcane farm. I remember two of my dogs always accompanied me and were at my side. The dogs were named Ranger, a brown dog, and Whitey, a white dog. They were my companions all day long, whether I was working or resting.

I would go to the farm and start to work early in the morning. It was better to start the work before sunrise while it was still comfortable to operate. Plowing the field was not easy, especially since it was all manual. There was no one to guide me, and I managed everything the best way that I could. I worked without shoes, wore a short-sleeved shirt and short pants. After a few hours of work, someone from the family would bring my breakfast. Most of the time, it was roti and potato curry with tea. There was enough food for me. I always had enough roti to share with my dogs. After breakfast, I would work for a few more hours, and when it became scorching hot I would stop work as the oxen needed time to rest, eat, and drink water. Of course, I as well needed to get some rest.

I would remove all the gears of the machinery and take the animals to the nearest river to drink water. Then I would find an area for them to graze. By then, it would be around noon and time to eat lunch. I do not remember how it was delivered to me or who delivered it. I only remembered that it was. When lunchtime was over, it was time to harness the bullocks again and go back to work. I would work on the farm until six PM and then head back home. By seven PM, we would arrive home. At home, my work was still not complete. I had to feed the animals and tie them down for the rest of the night. As for my dogs, we would go to the river and take a swim to clean up. We returned home for dinner, and after a good night's sleep, we started the process all over again.

We had three locations for the family farm. Two of the locations were mostly for sugarcane farming. The third area was in Nawaka. Here we had both residential as well as agricultural land. The significance of this location was that we had a combination of sugarcane and rice farming. At this location, since it was also our residence, we had all the necessary pieces of farming equipment and the animals used in cultivating the land. We did not have any automation. It was primarily due to not having financial means. When the time came to plant sugarcane, it required the support of all our family members, including other hands from our neighbors. My responsibilities included getting the soil ready for planting, depending on the season.

Chapter 33

SUGARCANE PLANTING *and* CARING FOR YOUNG PLANTS

WHEN IT WAS time to plant sugarcane, I would get the land ready. It meant that the area needed to be free from wild weeds, and the soil had to be very pliable and soft to create the proper environment. The planting of sugarcane required getting the right kind of seedlings. My father had the knowledge and the contact to get us the needed items. Once the decision got made for planting, I would get sugarcane seedlings delivered to the field. The seedling is required to be in strategic locations on the soil prepared for planting sugarcane.

Once all the necessary items were available, the next day, there would be as many as ten to fifteen people to assist in planting the sugarcane. Planting sugarcane was very different than rice planting in that it required arid land. Initially, with help from one of my brothers, I would prepare the ground for planting sugarcane. Once softened, tilling the land as necessary, we created rows about three feet wide. The furrows that we made were up to two hundred feet long and had to be very straight. This task was not easy, so someone with lots of experience had to do this. All of the future work required the rows to be straightforward and perfectly aligned. Once the furrows got created, a second person needed to place the sugarcane one by one in a line within the tracks. Since each sugarcane cut used to be about five feet long, they needed to be placed correctly in the rows. Once these were in place, a third person was required to cut the canes about six inches long while ensuring that each cutting had eyes at both ends. It was extremely critical, as germination started at those eyes. Once they cut the sugarcane in small (about seven to eight inches), the fourth person placed it in the soil and pressed down on it hard to ensure that the eyes were facing up. The fifth person then covered the cuttings with original soil before the furrows got created so that the eyes would grow properly. The covering could be up to six inches deep. The process required sufficient time for each row of planting to be done. Depending on the land's size, it took hours to complete the job. Since we had up to thirty acres of land, this process would take up to two weeks to finish the job. It was just the beginning of planting sugarcane. After planting, we hoped to get rain to allow the sugarcane to germinate. While we waited, the whole field of this new plantation needed protection from wild and domesticated animals that could damage the young growth. Sometimes it was necessary to fence the entire area to protect the young development from being eaten by local stray animals. We always needed to be on guard to make sure that nothing was damaged. I remember my dad used to plant a few beans within these furrows for an additional benefit. Since sugarcane took a long time to germinate, adding a few beans did not affect the new sugarcane growth.

The product of sugarcane farming, brown sugar, was widely used in Fiji. Everyone drank their tea with brown sugar. Brown sugar was also commonly used in making many varieties of Indian sweets. Thus, the sugarcane industry in Fiji was necessary for both local as well as global consumption. Another product that required sugarcane was liquor. Molasses, a by-product of sugar, is widely used in making rum. Sugarcane farming is a lengthy process. It takes up to a year for the first plant to harvest. After a few months, when the sugarcane plant had grown to about three feet, we fertilized the plant to ensure rapid growth. The fertilizer used was ammonium sulfate. We purchased the product from Colonial Sugar Refining Company (Fiji). The company began its operation in 1880 and ceased its operation in 1973.

Fertilizing these noticeably young plants was a very tedious process and needed several people to get it done. This fertilizer came in large sacks and was very expensive. My dad had a unique system made with wild pieces of lumber, with two thick wood pieces that could slide on the ground. A pair of oxen could then pull this special device. The fertilizer sacks would arrive by train on a specific day. I had to be ready to go to the railroad area close to our primary school that I used to attend to pick up these sacks. While waiting for the train, I would see my old classmates dressed in their uniforms going to high school while I stayed with my oxen to pick up the fertilizer. I used to be very embarrassed by my situation at the time. Especially since I was much better at my studies in school than many of the students now able to go to high school, these were challenging days for me, and I kept thinking of how I would give up farming.

Taking care of the growing plants took constant surveillance and maintenance. We needed to control the weed growth in the sugarcane field. Thus, we had to perform regular plowing in between the furrows to get rid of the wild weeds. And this was routinely done, which required extra help. Sometimes, I would fertilize the growing plants to help in their growth. Fertilizing the young plants is expensive both in terms of the fertilizer cost and the cost of labor.

Once the sugarcane had grown to maturity, it was time to be harvested. It was the final and potentially most rewarding phase for a farmer. All efforts in increasing the sugarcane were in the hands of the cane cutters. This task was laborious and required considerable effort and organizational skills to ensure that the harvested cane got safely to the mill for crushing.

My Brother Hari Narayan was always ready to do his duty. Cane cutting requires being manually done. He would get ready to leave home to the sugarcane farm around three in the morning. He would do this daily during the cane cutting season. My job was to make sure to get breakfast and lunch to him early in the morning. After delivering the food to him, I would then go to Andrews Government Primary School. It was challenging for me, especially when it rained, but this was one of my responsibilities, and I took it very seriously. The ladies needed to prepare the food early in the morning as well. My Brother Hari Narayan not only helped in growing the sugarcane, but he was also ready to cut the cane. We all counted on him to cut cane for our family. I remember him returning from the day's work when he required lots of massage due to cramps that developed. I felt deeply sorry to see his suffering.

Chapter 34

RICE PLANTING *and* HARVESTING

EVEN THOUGH I had the opportunity to work on other things than farming, I was always aware of my first responsibility. I was mindful of the seasonality of agriculture, and when the rainy season started, it was time to plant rice. Rice planting is much different from that of sugarcane farming in that rice planting requires lots of rain, significantly when growing rice from seedlings. Here I had to depend on my father, who would provide advice and support for getting ready.

After heavy rain, I would harness the oxen and hook them with a hanger. This particular device, when used properly, softens the soil. It had up to fifty long metal claws that, when dragged on the ground with one inch to two-plus inches of water, allowed the soil to become very muddy and liquid. The area must retain moisture, which means that the rainwater cannot run off the drainage system. While working within this area, I would be knee-deep in the soft soil. It was an ugly looking sight. Once the ground was ready, we would transplant rice seedlings six inches apart. The planting of rice seedlings also requires five-plus people. My mom, along with my sisters, would all help with this chore. This task was a family affair, and in this regard, we all wanted to contribute to getting the job done. This method of planting would yield much higher rice production than planting on dry soil. Since rice was our primary food source, my father wanted us to plant rice in dry soil. Growing rice on dry ground does not require much effort. My dad and I would get the rice planting done by just two of us on the dry land.

Rice planting, especially in muddy soil, is a filthy business. I recall an incident when my Bhabhi Irene was visiting us from Suva. Mrs. Irene Jai Narayan had just started teaching at a high school in Suva, Fiji. She later became a parliamentarian in the Fiji government. My brother, Jai Narayan, married her while he was in India. As she was from Suva, a city, it was a revelation for her to see how we planted rice. I had just returned from preparing the rice paddy. Because of the muddy soil, my legs were covered up to my knees with black mud. As I was taking off the harness from the oxen, Bhabhi Irene saw me and commented upon my appearance as "chi, chi, chi, Munna" ("stinky looking legs"). My legs almost looked like I had black boots on. It did look nasty, so she was right to make such a comment. Upon reflection, it was not a healthy way to do farming, but I did not know any better at the time. But rice planting, especially planting seedlings, required the soil to be very porous and moist for seedlings to stay firm in the ground. As to my name, it was a nickname. *Munna* is like a baby. Since

I am the youngest of my mother's children, it was an appropriate nickname.

Rice farming is dirty work at best; sugarcane farming is much cleaner and somewhat better. Both types of farming are hard labor. It was even more challenging for us because we had to do everything by hand. Both sugarcane farming as well as rice farming required many workers. It is beneficial to have a more prominent family, as the children could help with farming. Rice farming provides rice for the family, while sugarcane farming brings the family cash.

I remember the days when we all had to harvest the rice. It was very challenging to cut the rice plant and then separate the seeds from the plants. The ladies knew what was needed to extract the rice seeds from the plants. They would find a flat area in the field and lay down a layer of sack material about ten to fifteen feet wide. We would then get an ox or a horse to go over the plants to get the seeds out. This process was a whole-day affair. We needed to separate the seeds from the plant stem, which was a very tedious but slightly fun process. The goal was to extract the grain from the plant. The seeds were then left to dry out. We, of course, hoped for a very bright sun for those few days. Once the rice seeds were dried, we would put them in a sack and store them in a dry place. Many of us would stay around to fill the bag with the seeds for proper storage. Every so often, we would take the rice seeds out for drying under the sun. Once the seeds were dried, we would take the dried seeds to the mill to produce the rice. Most of the Indian families in Fiji took similar steps to grow rice. It was one of our principal foods; thus, it needed extra care. We used to harvest up to twenty sacks of rice per year, each weighing about sixty pounds.

Chapter 35

MY LIFE *on the* FARM

MY LIFE ON the cane fields was not a happy time for me. I was heartbroken about not being able to go to high school. Many of my classmates who were now able to go to high school felt superior to me. They began to distance themselves from me whenever we met, mainly when I visited Nadi Town. It caused me more pain and made me bitter about my life as a farmer. Farming, in general, did not make me feel proud. In general, we all were farmers in the village and did not think that people looked up to it. However, life had to go on as my options were limited due to the family situation. Once I began farming full-time, things started to unfold in that I realized that farming was not a full-time job. Thus, if they wanted to, a farmer could learn a trade while continuing to do farming. Once I realized this, I decided to begin to look for some other type of occupation.

My first thought was to try my hand as an auto mechanic. One of the main reasons for selecting this trade was that my Brother Ravindra Nath worked as an auto mechanic at a garage in Nadi Town. Also, one of my young friends from our village started to learn this trade as well. Since he was in a similar predicament as I was, it seemed reasonable for me to join him. Of course, I had to get approval from my family to undertake such a venture.

Chapter 36

THE FIRST DAY *at the* MECHANIC SHOP

ON MY FIRST day at the auto mechanic shop, I felt somewhat bewildered, for there was no one around to receive me. The mechanic shop was in the middle of Nadi Town, right across the road leading to the Nadi market. This shop did not have any specific teaching program, which meant that I would team up with one of the mechanics who would be my teacher for the day. There were three mechanics in the garage. The garage did not have a shop; thus, it was open to the elements. On the cement flooring, the mechanics created a workspace for under the cars. There was a bench along one side for tools and a small space for work. Mr. Hussain, the owner, was happy to have me at his garage. He instructed me about what to expect while I was at his shop. It was very plain and straightforward, and it became clear that there would not be much learning from the first day.

There were no benefits, nor was any money paid. I was the person who had to repair and change tires and perform lube jobs on all the cars. Also, the routine duty was to keep the garage clean and make sure that there would be no messy clutter around the work area. There was minimal teaching by the mechanics since they worked on special projects, such as how to troubleshoot the cause of a problem. It was essential to find the problem first then perform the repair work based on the problem identified. All troubleshooting took place based on trial and error. It was also dependent on the mechanic's experience. Even though I was not learning much about auto mechanics, I kept hoping that my learning ability would improve. On-the-job training was not to be, so after six months of this menial labor and with no opportunity to learn, I decided to leave the garage.

Although I did not gain much knowledge or pay for my efforts, I was determined to learn a trade other than just being a farmer. So, the next thing that I tried to delve into was carpentry. My Brother Shiu Narayan and a cousin were both carpenters. Both worked at Nadi Airport, which was about seven miles from our home in Nawaka. They both seemed happy with this trade, and it appeared to me that I as well could learn how to become a carpenter. My cousin's brother, Vidya Nath, was working for Fiji Builders at the Nadi Airport. He was more than happy to offer me a job at Fiji Builders. It was possible since he was the supervisor of this group at Nadi airport. Fiji Builders was, at the time, an Australian company that had a good reputation in Fiji. They would build single-family homes at the Nadi airport and around Nadi Town. I started to work, close to the airport, in an area known as the townhouse location. It was a beautiful site overlooking the Pacific Ocean. We were building the house for the manager of Qantas Airline. I felt overly excited about the prospect of learning carpentry, knowing that we would be working to build a home for a white man. For me, this was an opportunity to see in what type of home those white people would live in Fiji. The contrast between housing in the village and new construction built for a white person was huge. For example, just having running water, a toilet, and a shower room within the home was unique to me.

The commute to Nadi Airport was up to seven miles, which was a problem. Anyone working at Nadi Airport had to travel by bicycle or find some other type of transportation. I needed a bike like my cousin's brother. Since my Brother Deo Narayan still worked for Samji, I approached him to buy me a bike. Without hesitation, he promptly got me a new bicycle. It was such a lovely present that made me very happy. Brother Deo Narayan was always helpful to our family. He was an angel and made all of us grateful for his dedication to us. Now, with my bicycle, going to work was much more enjoyable. Riding on a bike was always a fun activity for us growing up in Fiji. A few of us worked at the Nadi airport, and since all had a bicycle, it was fun going together as a team.

When I started to work with Fiji Builders, learning to be a carpenter presented some challenges. One of the significant challenges was that I did not have the necessary tools. Thus, I was relegated to making tea and acting as an aide to the carpenters. Being an aide meant that I had to provide support to those who needed me to do things for the carpenters with anything related to building the house. It was acceptable to me since I was there to learn the carpentry trade. Of course, I saw this as a temporary situation, hoping that I would get an opportunity to be with carpenters who were willing to teach me. Being new to this trade, I had no idea what to expect. My cousin's brother used to tell me that it took time to become a carpenter. Since they did not have any training schools around us, I had very few options but to stick with on-the-job training.

There were days when I would leave home earlier than the others. Before showing up at the worksite, I would stop at the Natalis Shop to pick up an apple or pear, a real treat since these fruits were not available to us around our village. It was also interesting to see other fruits and vegetables that were not familiar. The store catered to mostly the local people; white people would also buy things from this store. I felt special to be able to buy stuff from the store. Since I was from a village environment, this experience opened my eyes to a different culture. Since I was always curious about learning new things, being around Nadi Airport was exciting. Everything seemed distant at the airport. Seeing the planes take off and land excited me, and seeing different people piqued my curiosity; thus, I wanted to learn more.

My hourly wage at work was fifteen pence an hour. Since I was in training, this seemed reasonable, and I was happy about earning some money. The foreman would ask me to make tea for the rest of the people most of the time. The money was good, though, so I kept this job for over six months. I still had to continue farming simultaneously, which was tough, but life was tolerable, and I had limited choices anyway.

PART IX:

STARTING *to* PLAN FOR MY FUTURE

Chapter 37

BEGINNING *to* FOCUS ON MY FUTURE

IT WAS IN 1955 when my Brother Jai Narayan returned from India to Fiji with his wife, Irene. He had been away for six years from our family for his studies and was the first in our family to complete a university education. Therefore, this was a proud moment for us. I remember the festive atmosphere at my uncle's home in Nadi Town, where there was a huge celebration for my brother and his wife. They had a tiny child with them, and everyone admired the little boy. Bhabhi Irene was new to our family, but she also had another little boy with her. It was a first for our family, having Bhabhi Irene and her son both born in India.

Interestingly, we now had family from India in Fiji without signing any contract like in the Girmitiya days. Seeing such a welcoming celebration for my brother, I kept thinking whether there would be any such opportunity for me as well. At the time, there was very little hope for me, especially since I did not have much schooling in Fiji. It was a constant reminder for me and it was very bothersome to look for a solution.

Our family in Nawaka also had a big welcome ceremony for my brother and his family. Most of the people in our village came to celebrate their homecoming. It was beautiful to see the family proud of their son, who had received a university degree. Not only was our family proud, but the village people all were proud as well. Seeing such excitement by all present, I was inspired to try to find a way so that I, as well, could accomplish something similar. I would feel sad to think about putting myself in a position to obtain a university education. All appeared exceedingly difficult, especially since I did not have a high school education, while the three brothers who had left for university had completed high school in Fiji. It appeared very remote for me, especially without a high school education, to even think of departing Fiji for higher education, and I would get very disheartened. It was tough being in a farming village, surrounded by teenage children, with minimal opportunity to excel in learning beyond a primary school education.

Since I continued to learn new things, it became clear that I must do something other than farming. But what would that be? It was not apparent, and very few could provide me with any direction. I do not remember talking with my Brother Jai Narayan about my future. Brother Jai and his family had little income since they were just starting in life. They had to move to Suva, Fiji's capital, for teaching positions at local high schools. He also had to repay all the money that Uncle Harry Prasad had spent on him. There was no one to look to for any support. Two of my other brothers were gone, one in India and the second in New Zealand. It was tough to get any answers to the questions about my future from anyone. I just had to keep working on the farm and hope my time would come at some point.

In the meantime, I began to look for some other trade besides farming that would be more suitable for my future. I suppose back then; I was looking for a position in an office. I was able to find training as a telephone operator at the Nadi post office. I did this in the evening shift, and it was a very convenient time to learn. I would complete my farming tasks and rush to the post office to train for this new job. Certainly it was the opportunity I was looking for, as I would later learn. This new system allowed me a chance to talk with people outside of Fiji. I never realized that there were other countries with people speaking different languages. I thought all the people with slanted eyes were Chinese. I must admit that I did not know that people were Japanese, Korean, or other Asian ethnicities. I also did not know much about Europe. My knowledge about geography and people from diverse cultures was minimal. While attempting to learn the technical aspect of the telephone, I was overly excited to learn about people from other parts of the world. It was the most exciting and significant learning situation that I found in the PBX Operator training program.

At this point in my life, it became apparent that being a farmer was not for me. Thus, I became more convinced than ever that I had to make my future a priority.

While farming was our occupation, and the primary reason for the Indian migration from India was for sugarcane cultivation, it was not for me. The simple fact is that the farmers seldom get recognized in the community. No one noticed you. You were just an ordinary person among many. I did not want to be like that. I yearned for education like my brothers. In 1956, I was fortunate that my brother, Prem Narayan, agreed to join us in Nawaka Village. Prem Narayan had stayed with Uncle Harry Prasad for about ten years. He was one of the last young men in our family to have stayed there for so many years. I was able to convince Prem Narayan to come and help us at our farm in Nawaka. Mother Changi did not support this idea, which made things much more difficult, but I insisted for him to join us. Prem Narayan was a good farmer, and our family knew that we would pay our bills quicker by having him. With support from our family, Prem was welcome to come home. My mother was concerned that Uncle Harry Prasad would find it exceedingly difficult not to have an extra hand helping him. Mother was very fond of my uncle and needed reassurance that we would support her favorite brother as required.

Chapter 38

UNCLE HARRY PRASAD

FROM MOTHER CHANGI'S perspective, Uncle Harry needed to have adequate help on his farm. Historically, my Uncle Harry always had one of my brothers at his home at any given time. This practice had started when the boys were as young as nine years old. One of the primary reasons my mother was very much obligated to Uncle Harry was that he helped her in times of need. More importantly, Uncle Harry did not have any boys of his own at the time and desperately needed help with his dairy and sugarcane farming.

My Brother Jai Narayan told me that he worked from incredibly early in the morning to late at night when he was at Uncle Harry's home. Uncle Harry was very clever and could apply his skills to make sure that all aspects of farming were profitable. Besides sugarcane farming, he also planted vegetables for the local market. As well, he started dairy farming and supplied milk to the townspeople. The last person to stay at Uncle Harry's was my Brother Prem Narayan. He and I were about the same age. While he was at Uncle Harry's, I often visited him. I got to know him well, and often we would go together to see movies. I would talk to him about my situation during these times, which he would sympathize with, but he could not do anything for me. After a while, it became apparent that he also was looking to join his family with ours in Nawaka. Brother Prem Narayan had already spent much more time at Uncle Harry's home than any other brothers in the past. Also, we in Nawaka Village were having issues with managing our farm. It was because I no longer wanted to do any farming. It was apparent that our family unity in Nawaka Village had become stressful. It was clear to me that Brother Prem Narayan had to come and join our family in Nawaka.

Chapter 39

AN OPPORTUNITY FOR ME *to* LEAVE FIJI

WHEN BROTHER PREM arrived in Nawaka, it was a gift from God. Suddenly, it became apparent that the time had come for me to start planning for my future. Kanchan Lodhia, a young boy from our village, had left for California in 1956. Kanchan's brother Kuman Lodhia and I had become excellent friends. We often got together during the late evening hours. It became a routine for us; thus, we would plan to meet after his shop closed for business. We would sit next to the Nawaka River and talk about our life in general. We always talked about our future and what it would be like to find a new type of work. Kuman ran his father's shop in our village and seemed to be inwardly happy.

On the other hand, I was not happy with my life at all. While sitting near the Nawaka River in the evening with bright moonlight, I dreamed of a different occupation. We would talk about America, India, Australia, New Zealand, and whether migration to these countries would ever be possible. Kuman suggested that I write to Kanchan in America for his advice. He provided me with Kanchan's address, and I wrote to him. Kanchan replied to my letter, a pleasant surprise, and suggested how I should go about getting the two recommendation letters and forms necessary for a student visa to America. It seemed possible suddenly that I could go to America!

I recall, I went back to work for Fiji Builders and was assigned to work on the Nadi Town Civic Center building. I was excited about the possibility of going to America and would mention my intentions to coworkers. Most of them would laugh and make jokes and often say that I was crazy. Most felt that this would never happen; of course, this encouraged me to prove them wrong.

I also started to talk with my family about my intent to leave Fiji. My dad would not want to hear of such a thing. He was against the idea. I had a tough time convincing him about my plan to leave Fiji. He was not convinced that I had sufficient experience, and I was only seventeen at the time. He commented that he would not sign any papers that I would need to get my documents from immigration for travel overseas. My mother was not thrilled about the idea, either. She did not want me to leave the family in Nawaka Village and felt saddened that I was her youngest son. She already had two of her sons who had left for studies overseas. However, it was apparent that my life in Fiji was a depressing one. I needed to follow three of my brothers who had left Fiji by going overseas to improve their future. The significant difference was that they already had completed a high school education, whereas I had not.

Chapter 40

NAWAKA FAMILY BREAKUP

OUR FAMILY LIVED together as a unit for many years. We all lived in a compound and ate meals cooked from the same kitchen under one roof. Although there was some indication that our family unit was about to break up, no one seriously thought such a thing could happen. But we all began to feel that it could be because I wanted to leave Fiji. Thus, breaking up the family unit could become a reality sooner rather than later. It is also possible that some of the brothers were feeling ambivalent about continuing to support the few of us who were seeking higher education, especially in my case, since I did not have a high school education. Also, there continued to be concern about the family farm. Who would take responsibility for planting, harvesting, and managing such an entity? These were some serious concerns, but I had made up my mind on beginning preparation to leave Fiji. However, what was to happen to our family unity, and what direction would the family take? Two of my brothers' kids were coming of age and were thinking of their interests and future. There were many unknowns within our family structure at the time. I felt responsible for creating such turmoil within our family. But it was also possible that the time had come for such a thing to happen. It is also true that our family had become significant, and living together was proving stressful. My brothers, who were married, now had their children, and they needed to think of their future. For those who were not married and did not have children, it did not matter as much.

Chapter 41

PROPERTY DIVISION *of the* NAWAKA FAMILY

IT HAS BEEN customary within the Indian community to call upon recognized leaders to divide property within the family unit. It is called Panchayat (a village council). This system has been used in India for generations and has proved to be highly effective in successfully resolving family disputes. Thus, it was not surprising that our Indian community in Fiji recognized the value of such a system and used it when there was a need to do so. As I understood it, when my maternal grandfather needed to settle his family disputes, he used the Panchayat system to help distribute his property. I am not sure if there was any input from those affected by adopting the Panchayat system, but no one could raise any issues. It is also true that no one was in any position to seek legal advice from lawyers at the time. In general, the eldest of the family agreed to use this system to settle the division of the property.

I distinctly remember the place and the protocol of the process. I am not sure of the details, but it was clear that there was significant tension among us regarding the property division. The reason for such uncertainty was rather apparent, for this was the first time such a dramatic issue needed addressing among the five elders in my family. I also needed my share to be in cash. I needed the money to buy my ticket to travel to America. I realized that the decision-makers would recognize my need. I knew that most, if not all, of my family members would be happy to support me. I felt that everyone would recognize my contribution to our family during the last four years on the farm and provide the necessary support to make our life better than before. More importantly, I had to sacrifice my education so that all would benefit from my efforts.

It was in the evening that a few community leaders had gathered in our largest Bure house. In one corner of the house was a sack full of rice, and in the middle was a long and strong post. The leader of the community sat next to the center. He was highly regarded within our village and had a great deal of experience in setting disputes.

The process began and was very civil and well organized. The Nawaka property, which was under my mother's name, had to be addressed first. The committee decided that the two brothers Deo Narayan and Shiu Narayan would share this property. My mother was to live with Brother Deo Narayan at the Nawaka compound as well. The tin house that my maternal grandfather built called "Dukan" would remain with my mother. What is a Dukan? It is a grocery shop that became our home after the renter left. Brother Shiu Narayan had his own house at the time in the Nawaka compound as well. He was a carpenter and worked at the Nadi airport. Brother Hari Narayan had his place in the Nawaka compound as well. The committee additionally granted five acres of sugarcane farming land across the river. My father and his own family were awarded the land in Tongo, across the river to Brother Hari Narayan. Brother Prem Narayan was to live with my father. There was some controversy about this property since this was the wealthiest sugarcane farming property awarded to Brother Deo Narayan. He did not feel right about this award and gave the Tongo land to my father. Deo Narayan was a very compassionate man, and this was an example of his character. He also was known for his kindness, generosity, and honesty in our family.

The Panchayat system worked, and all felt comfortable with the results. Of course, I was selfish and not much concerned about others' issues and concerns. My main problem was getting the cash I needed. I needed the money urgently since all necessary documents for my trip to the United States had been completed. The only thing remaining was to obtain my passport and travel ticket for my journey.

Shiu Nath, my brother-in-law, loaned me the money that I needed to buy my ticket. His younger brother was married to my sister Tara Wati. One thing that was significant about Shiu Nath was his loyalty and dedication to helping anyone in need. He was an enormously proud man and always stood up for our family. I do not remember who was responsible for paying him back the money loaned me. I learned later, in fact after my first return to Fiji, that this money was paid back to him by my Brother Hari Narayan. Brother Hari was a straightforward person, and he was around to help me. Brother Hari and I worked side by side in farming. I remember days when he used to harvest sugarcane. He used to leave home early in the morning without any food, which I had to deliver to him daily. There were times where this task was arduous, especially during the rainy seasons. But no matter the difficulties, I would consistently have his breakfast and lunch before going to school. Brother Hari was committed to providing the needed support for all of us. God blessed both Mr. Shiu Nath and Brother Hari Narayan for their help when I needed it the most.

After I had the cash, I took a leave from work and boarded a bus to Suva to get my passport and ticket. The Pacific Bus Service operated daily, and I wanted to be on time to catch the bus to travel to Suva, Fiji's capital city. It took up to four hours to travel from Nadi to Suva. It was an arduous bus ride via a gravel road. Traveling by bus to Suva made me sick, and I often vomited while the bus continued moving. It was extremely uncomfortable as well as embarrassing. Traveling to Suva was important for us. It was uncommon for most of us from our village to take such a trip.

After about four hours on the bus, I arrived in Suva and found the necessary documents. It was my second trip to Suva, and lots of things were new and very strange. I was delighted to get the required documents without much difficulty.

Now the problem was how to get back home. I decided to visit my Brother Jai Narayan's home to seek his advice. My dilemma was about how to return to Nadi since the bus service to Nadi had already left. My brother was willing to drive me to Nadi, but Bhabhi Irene objected to this solution. Besides, this idea of going back to Nadi was not practical because of the distance from Suva to Nadi. Also, it would have been tough for my brother on the return trip from Nadi to Suva during the night. The round trip would have taken a minimum of six to seven hours, and upon his return, he would be driving back alone. I understood Bhabhi's issues and was very sympathetic to her concerns. She was concerned on two levels. One was that Brother Jai had to teach school the next day, but also, she would be alone with her son with no one to provide child-care support. Additionally, they were just getting started with their life in Fiji. It shows how difficult it must have been for Bhabhi Irene to transition from India to the Fiji Islands.

Brother Jai Narayan dropped me at the bus station that was going from Suva to Sigatoka. I bought the ticket and traveled to Sigatoka and from there took a cab to Nadi. I guess I must have had some extra money for the taxi fare. I also remember buying some local crab from the roadside to celebrate my getting the traveling document ticket and the passport. I arrived in Nadi just in time for dinner. Badki Bhabhi prepared crab curry, and we enjoyed the meal.

The next day was going to be my last day with my family in Nawaka. My mother was a very religious person who wanted to have a short prayer service in the evening. She had invited a few family members and some of my close friends for this service. I do remember many had come to wish me luck for my future. I spent my last night in Fiji with family and friends. The next day, we were to depart for Suva. There were lots of mixed emotions and feelings. The reality was setting in that this was the last time that I would see my family and friends for years to come, if ever again. As I looked at those around me in the car, everyone looked sad and was noticeably quiet, not knowing what to say. Since we were nearing one of my sisters' homes, I asked to take a break and take a few minutes to visit her.

It was still morning, and we stopped the car and went into the compound to say hello. My sister Kamala Wati was speechless to see me. She lived in Cuvu. It was nice to see her. Sister Kamala was pleased to see us and was surprised that I was leaving Fiji. It was also a lovely break from our long journey from Nadi. After a few minutes, we had to say goodbye; we got in the taxi and left for Suva. I was in the car with my mother, my Sister Utra, and my dad. It was a challenging trip for all, especially for my mother. It was difficult for me as well. My mother was crying on the way to Suva. I, as well, was very emotional and frankly not sure if what I was doing was the right thing.

PART X:

TRAVELING *on the* SHIP TO CALIFORNIA

Chapter 42

SS ORSOVA

WE ARRIVED IN Suva, and the ship, the *SS Orsova*, looked huge. After I saw the ship, it became authentic that my dream was becoming a reality. I saw the travelers getting in and out of the ship in a great mood; they all seemed happy. On the other hand, I was not pleased and felt incredibly sad about saying goodbye to those in attendance at the harbor. My brothers Deo Narayan, Shiu Narayan, Jai Narayan, Prem Narayan, my sister Utra Kumari, Bhabhi Irene, Uncle Harry Prasad, and a few friends were there to see me off to America. They all as well were sad to see me getting ready to leave Fiji. While saying goodbye to all, someone from the ship called out my name on the speaker. Bhabhi Irene yelled out to let me know that I had to get on board quickly before it started to move out of the dock. Bhabhi Irene knew about these things since she had just arrived from India by ship. Boarding the boat was a challenging moment for me. Saying goodbye to my mother was very painful for me. I tried to assure her that everything would be okay and acceptable and that I would often communicate with the family.

All I remember is getting on the ship and trying to find my way around the crowd. One of the aides took me down to my cabin, which was on the lowest bottom deck. There were six bunk beds in the cabin, and I was the only one in the place. I sat on the lowest bunk and began to cry. I felt very lonely and confused. Suddenly, I heard the ship's siren and went running to the main deck to get to see my mom and the rest of the family. I remember having a white handkerchief and beginning to wave to those I was leaving behind. The ship started to move and slowly but surely began to gain speed. I still remember waving the handkerchief until all became invisible. Indeed, it was a sad day for all of us, especially for me, for I was not sure about the unknowns of my future.

Chapter 43

MY FIRST DAY *on the* SHIP

AS THE SHIP continued moving farther away from the harbor, it became apparent that I might not see any of my family members for a long time. This thought brought tremendous sadness, and I felt very much alone standing on the deck of the ship. All I saw now was the ocean and no sign of any life for as far as my eye could see. The realization of being alone without my mom and the rest of my family made me very sad, but there was not much to do but cautiously try to find my way down to the lower deck and find my room. Being alone, I felt very isolated and began to cry. There was no one to counsel me nor provide any comfort. It was not too long before I fell asleep on the lowest bunk bed in the cabin. There was no one else in the room except me. I didn't know why I was alone in the place. I guess it may have been because I got the cheapest room on the ship.

Soon it was apparent that it was time for dinner. I had no idea where to go. It was getting dark, but all the indoor lights were on, so I stepped out of the cabin to investigate my surroundings. While walking around, I felt dizzy and quickly returned to my room. I was feeling seasick and began to throw up. I very quickly changed my clothes and got into bed and fell asleep. It was tranquil in the cabin; unlike the way it was in my village life.

The following day, I got up and looked for the bathroom right next to my cabin. All around the toilet were systems I was unfamiliar with in the restroom area or when using the toilet. The toilet facility was hugely different from what I was familiar with in our village. It was a challenge and required some time to figure out how it worked. I needed to take a shower and had to learn the hard way. I was also not familiar with how to use the shower system and, while trying to shower, turned on the hot water and burned my back. It was not long before I was able to learn how to operate the shower and the toilet. It became apparent that to become familiar with this unfamiliar environment, I would need to find my way around. I did manage to find the cafeteria but was reluctant to go inside. I was not familiar with what to expect since, all my life, I had been with Indian people in our village and had never shared a meal with white people.

Moreover, I was not familiar with having to eat in a restaurant. Here I was among the white people and felt apprehensive about how to approach them. Besides, I still felt dizzy, lightheaded, and decided to pick up a menu to learn what I could eat while on this ship. Since I did not eat beef or pork, I needed to find the proper food. I was able to find lots of fruit to eat. It was delightful to be able to eat apples, bananas, grapes, papaya, and pineapple, as well as a few other kinds of fruit that I was not familiar with but was willing to try. Although these fruits were available, I could not eat much due to being seasick most of the time.

On the third day aboard the ship, I got out of my deck and explored the boat, visiting the different tiers. From these decks, all I could see was water all around me. There was no sign of any life outside. Our ship was sailing smoothly to our destination. We were on our way to Honolulu, our very first stop.

I was still seasick and not feeling well at all. Eating was out of the question since I was not able to keep anything in my stomach. Feeling sick all the time and not knowing what to do, I would often return to my cabin and rest. I do not remember eating much during my first few days, but I could load up on fruits to take to my place. It was always a treat, and I would enjoy these regularly when I was able to eat.

On my fourth day, I decided to have breakfast. I got out of bed, took a shower, dressed up appropriately, and went for my very first breakfast on the ship. I went to the eating area and found an empty table to sit down at. The waiter came and asked me for my order. I did not know how and what to order. I felt relieved since it was the first time a white person had asked me, very politely, what I wanted to eat. I found this to be quite different than what my life was as a farmer in Fiji. I asked for a poached egg with toast and coffee. Frankly, I did not know what else to order since many things on the menu were unfamiliar to me.

The atmosphere in the cafeteria was very relaxing. I felt wonderfully comfortable to be sitting with all the white people in an immaculate room. Suddenly, I felt important. I tried to eat but could not. I felt sick and went back to my cabin. As soon as I came back to my place, I could not keep much in my stomach and vomited whatever there was. After some rest, I went up to the deck, found a comfortable table, and sat down. A few minutes later, an elderly lady joined me and began to talk with me. She seemed interested in me and asked very politely the county I came from and my name. I was happy to respond. After a short conversation, I found her taking me to the doctor's office close to us. I was pleased with her assistance and thanked her for her kindness. The doctor provided me with some motion sickness tablets. He gave me specific instructions on when and how to take medicine. After taking medication, my life changed on the ship. I began to eat well, primarily fruits, bread, and coffee. Life on board the vessel was getting better. I could go to the library and the sports room. I tried playing badminton and felt good as I began to meet people. I still have a diary with some interesting autographs from people that I met on the *Orsova.* I find it interesting to read some of the things people that I met wrote. It is good to read some of the notes occasionally, whenever I can.

Chapter 44

FOURTEEN DAYS *on* *ORSOVA*

ONCE I OVERCAME my seasickness, I could move comfortably around the ship and began to enjoy the voyage. Our ship arrived in Honolulu on the morning of the seventh day of sailing from Fiji. I was not allowed to disembark the boat, I am not sure of the reason, but maybe it was because I was traveling on a student visa. There was a lot of activity on the ship. Some people were getting off and some were coming on board.

I believe we had docked for just a day, and soon it was time to depart from Honolulu. By now, I was getting used to eating food and meeting with people on the ship. I met an elderly gentleman who had just boarded the boat. Mr. Cole was from Canada. He was returning home from his short vacation in Honolulu. We became friends very quickly and began to see each other often. He was a very kind gentleman and took a particular interest in my welfare. When we arrived in Vancouver, Canada, he took me to have lunch with his family at his home. Mr. Cole's family lived on Marine Drive. I distinctly remember the place because of its beautiful location along the coast of Vancouver. I remember the served lunch, which included the following:

mashed potatoes, corn, bacon, and pork. The mashed potatoes were new to me, but I did not have trouble eating them. On the other hand, bacon and pork were not vegetarian, and I did not eat them. I remember that I apologized for not eating the entire lunch and hoped that they understood.

We had limited time in Canada and had to leave his home soon after lunch. One of his children drove me to the ship. It was time for us to sail again. It was in the evening we began to move away from the dock. The scene was gorgeous. The ship passed under the Lion's Gate Bridge, and soon we could see the City of Vancouver. It was like Diwali, the Hindu Festival of Lights, as there were lights all around us. Soon we were away from civilization, and there was smooth sailing toward our final destination, the state of California in the United States of America.

Chapter 45.

ARRIVAL *in* AMERICA

IT WAS EARLY morning when we saw land from a distance. One of the most memorable sights was the famous Golden Gate Bridge. I had heard some of the travelers on the ship talk about this bridge as vital since it was the main entrance to San Francisco. It was exciting to see the Golden Gate Bridge and for us to pass under the bridge, slowly moving toward the San Francisco harbor. We could also see the San Francisco Bay Bridge before docking on Pier 35. There was a lot of commotion on the ship before docking. People were hurrying back and forth, getting their bags and the necessary documents to get ready to disembark. I, of course, was anxious as well. I had already packed my suitcase, but I did not have much except a few souvenirs from Fiji that Kanchan had requested. I was relieved to see Kanchan and one of his American friends waiting for me on the dock. My excitement soon diminished when I was not allowed to disembark. The American immigration officer would not let me leave the ship. The reason given to me was that I was missing a vital medical document. American immigration required proof of syphilis serology clearance, which I did not have. I was not aware of this requirement. I am not sure if the syphilis serology test was made available for us in Fiji. Also, I am not confident about performing the test in Fiji. Those who had traveled before me did not know of this requirement. We were amazed to find this out. I did not know of such a policy, thus it was a surprise turn of events.

Mr. Finley, Kanchan's colleague, was allowed to come on the ship to help clarify what was needed. The U.S. Immigration Service allowed one of the officers from the ship to accompany me. Mr. Finley and Kanchan went with me to the U.S. Naval Hospital for an examination and a blood test, specifically the syphilis serology test. Once this test was done, I got a two-week visa as I waited for the test result. Upon test completion, the result came out negative, meaning that I did not have syphilis. I was able to get my student visa for one year.

I was relieved to get the medical issue resolved. If this issue persisted, the Immigration Department would have sent me back to Fiji. It is essential to recognize the support and assistance of Mr. Finley. The mere fact he was there with me helped secure my entrance to the United States of America. The U.S. Department of Immigration recognized Mr. Finley's stature in giving me the pass. Once I was allowed to disembark from the ship, Kanchan drove me to Berkeley. It would be my residence for the next few months.

I distinctly remember Kanchan driving me on the Bay Bridge. While on the Bay Bridge, I could see the ship that had just brought me to San Francisco. All of these new experiences were exciting as well as overwhelming—everything looked so big. After going on the bridge, we got on Highway 101, the freeway. I also remember us taking the exit to Ashby Avenue. One of the most striking scenes for me was to see some Black children as we passed by a school. I noticed the English language spoken very differently than we spoke in Fiji. I inquired with Kanchan if these people were Americans. I am not sure what his response was, but it was a fascinating observation for me.

Kanchan had arranged for me to stay with him at 2310 Bowditch Street in Berkeley. He and I shared a room with two beds and a couple of tables to use in our studies. There was a shared bathroom that all of us used, as well as a shared kitchen. The apartment was small but extremely comfortable. There were a few Korean students and one American person. Of course, the kitchen had a refrigerator, a small stove, and a table with four chairs. I was informed of my responsibilities with kitchen maintenance, in that we were to take turns making sure that the kitchen was always kept neat and clean.

Across Bowditch Street was a Lutheran Church where we could go to play games and relax. Most important for me was that Kanchan could get me a job on the first day I arrived in the United States.

PART XI:

2310 BOWDITCH STREET, BERKELEY, CALIFORNIA

Chapter 46

MY VERY FIRST JOB *in* AMERICA

MY JOB AT the student boarding house was to peel sacks of potatoes and clean up vegetables. The boarding house owner would pick up old vegetables from the local markets and bring these for use at her boarding house. These vegetables were primarily good, but they were old and required picking the good from the bad ones.

In return for my work, I was to get breakfast and dinner. I was on my own for lunch. I do not recall eating lunch for several months since it was not an option. My friend Kanchan, in the meantime, worked in the kitchen. His primary responsibility was washing dishes. I was amazed to see him washing dishes to earn a living since this work was for ladies in Fiji. Most boys never did any job in the kitchen. Kitchen duties were the responsibility of women. I do not remember having any conversation with Kanchan about such tasks. However, it became clear after a few days that for us to make a living, we would do any type of honest work. You see, we were on our own; there was neither support from our family nor any help from any other sources. We were students, and as such, it was necessary to make a living and continue to pursue our education. So, washing dishes and cleaning up vegetables were essential steps toward improving our future. The future was our focus, and adjusting to make a living in the States currently was necessary.

Being independent was very inviting, and life was much more accessible here in the States than in Fiji, living in a village with a farming community. There was nothing wrong with being a farmer, but there was no future for the young without much education.

Chapter 47

THE BEGINNING *of* MY LIFE *in the* USA

MY LIFE IN the States began at 2310 Bowditch Street in Berkeley. I was very fortunate to have Kanchan to look after me and guide me as needed. He was like a big brother and made sure that I did the right thing. Having him around me was a great support, especially ensuring that I followed the proper path in this unfamiliar environment. We drove around Berkeley, and he introduced me to a few of Fiji's Indian families. One such family was Basil Rao and his wife. They lived nearby our apartment. They were very kind to us and would invite us on some special occasions for an Indian meal. It was great to be with them and enjoy real Indian family food—a real treat since we did not get to eat much Indian food for weeks.

Mr. Basil Rao, his wife, and two of his brothers lived in Berkeley. Basil worked for the Chef Boyardee company in San Leandro. He was later very helpful in getting me employed at this company on the evening shift. It was perfect for summer employment when I needed to earn a few extra dollars. I began working for this company much later in the year since I did not have transportation.

I also met a few Fijian boys who had come earlier to do their studies here in the States. Kanti Lal attended the University of California at Berkley, and Mohammad Yasin and Satya Narayan attended San Francisco State University. I was in good company and felt motivated to seek higher education just like these students. Most significant was that we used to get together and cook Indian food and socialize. Gathering in this way would provide a great relief, for I used to get very lonely being away from my family in Fiji. Of course, we were all in the same boat, so it was suitable for all of us to share our everyday issues. We used to socialize with a couple of other boys from Fiji, but they differed from our regular group. It was because of their lack of interest in attending school. Also, I and Kanchan were determined to be available to study and earn money for our rent and pay the necessary bills.

Chapter 48

MR. ALLEN FINLEY

OFFICER FINLEY HAD an office on Durant Avenue in Berkeley, not far from our apartment. He and his staff were involved with the Presbyterian church. I remember visiting his office often as this also provided an opportunity to talk about life in general. Pauline was his administrative assistant and was genuinely nice to all of us. She was always available to help us with any issues and concerns.

Kanchan and I regularly attended Presbyterian Church on Sundays. We were regulars at the social events, which were church-sponsored activities. I recall meeting a young lady who was my first date in this country. She attended Berkeley and lived in a sorority house near to where I lived. We became good friends during church services. By now, I had learned about some of the social norms for younger people. One of the things was about asking a girl for a date. I was not familiar with dating formalities, nor how to approach someone for a date. Not having transportation was also a hindrance. Since Diane and I used to see each other on a regular basis, I felt comfortable asking her for a date. So, after one of the church services, I asked her if she would like to go out with me. She agreed, and I was excited but nervous to meet her at her sorority house. On the day of our agreed-upon time to meet, I walked down to the sorority house and pressed the doorbell.

The door opened, and there she was, looking lovely and smiling in greeting. The first question was where we were going. I asked, "Where do you want to go?" And she said, "How about the donut shop right there?" I was pleased, and we went to the donut and coffee shop, close to the sorority house where she lived. It was clear that she knew about my situation and wanted me to be comfortable in the few hours together. She knew that I was very new to the country and was unfamiliar with the social norms—my first experience in the Western dating scene, which must have been evident to her. After the usual small talk, the server came and asked for our orders. Before I could say anything, she said that we would like coffee and a couple of donuts. I was relieved and felt at ease, knowing that she was very aware of my being nervous and very new to being alone with her for the first time. I found her to be very kind and gentle with me and the time spent together was a gratifying experience for me. After the coffee and donuts, I paid the bill, and we went for a brief walk around the block. It was getting late, so I dropped her at the sorority house, ensuring she was home safely. During the next few weeks, we kept in touch and often had a telephone conversation. We, of course, saw each other on Sundays during church services. We liked each other and often met for donuts and coffee at what became our regular hang out.

By now, I was getting very familiar with my surroundings and was getting well-adjusted to McKinley Adult School. It was not easy for me to start seeing other girls from high school regularly. I had many opportunities to meet other young women at various social events but felt uncomfortable asking for dates. Furthermore, I did not have transportation, nor did I have much money to ask them out. Dates were costly, and I did not have much money to spend.

Living on Bowditch Street was a real treat. It was close to Berkeley High School and the University of California. It was also close to McKinley Adult High School. I used to walk down to school from my apartment.

I owe much to McKinley Adult School for allowing me to come to America. It also provided me with my academic start and prepared me to get admitted to college. Kanchan had already attended this high school and was very familiar with the system, making my life much easier.

I started McKinley Adult High School in the Spring of 1957. Starting school after being out of such a system was a challenging adjustment. The idea of sitting in a classroom with other students was not extremely comfortable. It was especially true since much of the student body was from different countries. Also, many local students were not interested in attending this school. It was because they had difficulties with going to a regular high school.

On the other hand, I was overly excited to be in the classroom and wanted to learn as much as I could. I felt extremely comfortable being in the school and appreciated the teacher's willingness to teach us. My first subjects were English, mathematics, geography, typing, and American history. We had a different teacher for each subject, which I found very exciting. I thoroughly enjoyed learning as much as I could. I could not wait to go back to school and learn new things daily. The teachers were accommodating and kind. They were always available to provide a helping hand. My first semester at school went very well. I had all A's in my classes. Having done extremely well in my classes provided extra incentive to excel in academia in the future. The teachers were also very encouraging in making sure that I continued to do well in the future.

There was not much time to do anything else while going to school and working at the student boarding house for my meals. I also had to work for different families doing gardening on the weekends. The money earned would pay for my rent, which was $45 per month. Even though it was a particularly challenging year, I thoroughly enjoyed being in America and looked forward to schooling to make a better life for myself.

Chapter 49

DR. WILLIAM STILES

I OWE A lot to Kanchan for all his help and support. He not only helped me to come to America. He was always available to guide me in doing the right thing. Both of us were looking for ways to earn money to pay for the rent and some pocket change. Kanchan suggested that I advertise in a local newspaper as follows: "Foreign student looking for odd jobs." I must admit advertising for the job worked well for me to get lots of gardening work on the weekends. It turned out that it was one of the most productive things that I had done. These ads were a godsend, and within a few days, I had lined up more than three jobs. Two were for gardening, and the third was for gardening as well as some carpentry work.

The gardening work was for a couple of ladies. Both ladies lived in Berkeley but required me to take the bus to their homes. Taking a bus presented a challenge for me since I had never taken a bus before. However, I managed to find my way to go to work for them. Gardening was not challenging work for me since I had experience in farming in Fiji. The ladies were charming to me and were pleased with my work. They were impressed that I was able to get lots of work done within eight hours. I got paid $1.25 per hour, plus lunch. This type of work was suitable. I was delighted with getting paid enough to cover the cost-of-living expenses plus extra for some enjoyment while continuing my studies at McKinley Adult High School. It did not take me too long before I had adjusted well to my life in the States. I had turned eighteen during my first year in the States and felt absolute freedom to socialize. Now there was enough money for rent as well as money to spend to have good times. However, I needed to think about what to do during the summer months. Here is where Dr. William Stiles comes to mind.

Dr. William Stiles had called me and asked me to work for him on a somewhat regular basis. I was excited to work for him since there was not only gardening but also some carpentry work that I could do. Dr. Stiles worked for U.C. Berkeley in the Public Health department. I liked the opportunity of working for him for many reasons. First, he was willing to pick me up from my apartment on Bowditch Street in Berkeley and drop me back after work. The system worked well for me, especially since I did not have to wait and spend money on the bus fare. I started my career for Dr. Stiles initially on weekends and holidays. He would drive from El Cerrito in the early morning to pick me up and take me to his home to work in his yard. He had a big yard with fruit trees and lots of vegetation. After we arrived at his home, I met Mrs. Stiles, his wife, and two daughters.

They were very welcoming and made me feel very comfortable. Dr. Stiles showed me around and provided me with the necessary tools for work. Most of the gardening work was up the hill, which required extra effort to get the job done. Besides, he also had a small home on the property. I had to work around this property as well. After about four hours of work, Mrs. Stiles prepared lunch for me and invited me to her kitchen to eat. I felt uncomfortable but accepted the invitation. After a decent lunch, I went back to work and completed everything required for me to do.

It was getting late, and Dr. Stiles brought me back to my apartment. While driving back from work, Dr. Stiles said he was interested in me and wanted to know about my plans. It was clear that he wanted me to work for him on a regular basis. I was happy to see that he was pleased with my work and was willing to help me in the future. I worked extremely hard for Dr. Stiles with all the yard work. For all the work I did for Dr. Stiles, I got paid $1.25 per hour. I was delighted with the money.

It became evident that I could continue to work for just Dr. Stiles as needed and did not need to work for anyone else. I remember working for him on a full-time basis during the summer months. It was because he had decided to build a unit attached to his home. We had to dig the ground with hand tools to make this unit, creating enough space for a basement. I had to dig up the dirt by hand to create sufficient space for such construction. The soil that I removed had to be carried away up to thirty yards uphill in a wheelbarrow. It was a challenge and required lots of demanding work.

I remember telling Kanchan about the type of work that I had to do. Kanchan needed a job, and I asked Dr. Stiles to work with me on this project. Once Bill Stiles hired him, Kanchan and I worked together regularly. We would dig the ground and take turns carrying the soil uphill. It was a rewarding experience for both of us. I was surprised and pleased to see Kanchan worked as hard as I did. It was because Kanchan did not work on a farm in Fiji. He worked in his fathers' grocery shop. Gujrati's, the ethnic group that Kanchan belonged to, are not known to work this hard in Fiji. They primarily operated retail shops in Fiji, which is considered low manual labor.

When we completed digging, Bill Stiles did most of the carpentry work. Since I had done some carpentry in Fiji, I was able to help him with this chore. We managed to complete the construction project during the summer of 1958.

My next primary task was to put a new roof on Dr. Stiles' main home. I found this to be a challenge. I had done some roofing work in Fiji but was not familiar with tile roofing. Dr. Stiles showed me the proper technique, and I was able to finish the roofing efficiently.

The third major work that I did for Bill was digging a trench around the house. I had to dig a four-foot-deep by two-foot-wide trench all around the house. It was necessary because the house was on a hill, and drainage was of primary concern.

It so happened that Elaine Levesque had similar problems with her home. Seeing my work at Bill's house, she asked me to do some work at her home. I was ready to do the job, but I felt a need to ask Dr. Stiles' permission. Of course, he was willing for me to work on Elaine's yard as needed. This arrangement was a piece of good news for me since it almost guaranteed my employment regularly. Both Mrs. Levesque and Dr. Stiles lived on a cul-de-sac street, and the word had gotten around about me in that I was an extremely hard worker and would garden at a very reasonable cost. In this regard, a few other neighbors asked me about helping them as well. While working for Dr. Stiles, Mrs. Elaine Levesque, his neighbor, would observe my work. She expressed interest in me and asked Bill if I could do some gardening for her as well. Not only was she impressed with my work at Dr. Stiles' home, but she also was concerned about my character. It was vital for her safety since she lived alone. Now I had guaranteed work from both of these two people. Elaine liked my work and began to use me often. She also had friends that needed gardening work as well. Thus, for the time being, I had enough gardening to do on the weekends. I would earn enough money for rent and also be able to open a bank account. I was excited about the possibilities of the extra work as well as the options for my future.

Chapter 50

MR. NED REED

EVEN THOUGH THERE was enough work doing gardening, I needed to get work for the summer months. Kanchan and I continued to live together at Bowditch Street in Berkeley. We both were determined to do our best to work hard and continue to excel in school. By now, I had already completed my first year of high school and had become familiar with my surroundings. Kanchan worked for Mr. Reed during the summer months. Mr. Reed, a college teacher, owned a few residential buildings in Berkeley and Oakland. He needed lots of work done to his buildings, which was painting. Since Mr. Reed had several rental properties, he always had enough work for both of us. There was always work since the renters vacated. Potential new renters were looking for availability. We used to do general cleaning, change carpets and floors for new renters, and more. Mr. Reed was a junior college professor but had become a very successful landlord both in Oakland and in Berkeley. He was a very clever person when it came to taking care of his properties. During one of the summers, he had two university students from other states work for him. These two workers mostly did house painting for him, while Kanchan and I would do all the different jobs, including gardening.

When the time came to pay us for our efforts, he decided to pay me less than Kanchan. It was not okay with me, and I demanded to get paid at the same rate. Initially, he was reluctant to do so. However, after much discussion, he agreed to pay me the same as Kanchan. Our relationship after this became somewhat strained, but he still wanted me to continue to work for him. I continued to stay in Berkeley during my McKinley High School days. The property owners were genuinely nice to us, and our stay at the apartment was extremely comfortable. After one and a half years at McKinley Adult High School in Berkeley, it was apparent that the time had come for me to look at other schooling systems. Some of the teachers encouraged me to apply to study at a junior college. My high school grades were decent, so I was inspired to go to college rather than look for a job like an auto mechanic. Besides, I did not get much out of going to the evening classes at Berkeley High School to learn about being a mechanic. I was excited about the prospect of going to college, but where? I had heard of Contra Costa Junior College, located in San Pablo in Richmond. One of my terrific friends, Kanti Patel, helped me with the application and the necessary documents to submit to the college. I applied to the college; it was a waiting time. I needed to get accepted to this college within a month. It was because I needed to renew my student visa to continue staying in the country. I could not renew my student visa without the official acceptance letter from the college. To my surprise, I received an admission letter from Contra Costa College. With this in my hand, I got to stay in the country for another year. Additionally, getting accepted to the junior college with only one and a half years of high school was a morale booster. It was a real blessing, and I felt the future looked brighter for me moving forward.

Now I had to face some new challenges. The first concern was about finding a place to stay, which was a significant issue. Also, getting to college meant finding a place to stay where going to school would be convenient. Transportation was a big issue; thus, getting closer to the college would be necessary. Since I was still involved with the Presbyterian Church and continued to stay in touch with Mr. Finley, they helped me get located with one of the ladies from the church. This lady lived in the Richmond District, closer to the college. She lived with her two sons in a small house. She offered to help me until I got better situated. She also had an older son who lived in El Sobrante.

PART XII:

MOVE *to* RICHMOND *from* BERKELEY

Chapter 51

MY FIRST YEAR *at* CCJC *in* RICHMOND

I FEEL TRULY fortunate to have had some extraordinary Americans who supported me at every turn in my life. Of course, Mr. and Mrs. Finley were always there for me. I wish I had kept the names of those who were always available to support me, especially while making this meaningful change.

The day had arrived for me to move out of Berkeley to my new location. I did not have much to take with me but still needed transportation to move. As always, Kanchan, Satya, and Yasin helped me move. Yasin and Satya lived with families in Hillsborough, but still, they took the time to assist me with my move to Richmond. I shared a room with one of the families' youngest son, who was attending Richmond High School. It was genuinely nice of him to welcome me and help show me around the city. He showed me how to get to Contra Costa College by bus. The first day of school was challenging, but I got to school in time to attend my classes.

I stayed with this family for about two weeks but had to move to a new location. The older son and his wife lived in

El Sobrante, much further away from the junior college. Jerry, the older son, was married and had a young baby boy. I moved in with Jerry and his wife in El Sobrante. They had much better accommodation, which I think was the main reason for my move from Jerry's mother's home. I felt good staying with the family. They were genuinely nice to me and made every effort to make my stay with them extremely comfortable. They were generous enough to accept me in their home, especially since they started their new life together. The college was some distance from their home. I am not sure how I was able to get to college regularly. El Sobrante was a newly developed area, so the homes were primarily new. The house was away from the main town, thus was inconvenient for shopping. Since I was on room and board status, my duties included keeping the garage and the yard clean. I also had to vacuum the home, clean dishes after dinner, and look after the little one when needed. It was difficult for me to get to school and back home. But life, in general, was acceptable.

Chapter 52

EL SOBRANTE FAMILY HOME

I COULD NOT stay long at Jerry's home for several reasons: one of which was the commuting issue. It was a challenge to get to my college from there. Also, being with a young and newly married couple with a newborn baby was uncomfortable for me. The most crucial issue was that I needed to earn money; I continued gardening for Elaine. During my days at Elaine's, I would talk to Elaine about my challenges while staying at Jerry's home. Elaine was very sympathetic to my concerns and offered me room and board at her home. Elaine lived alone, and moving in with her would be of significant help to her and me as well. Besides, since Elaine was a schoolteacher, I felt this would benefit me while going to college. I would still have a long commute to the college by consenting to live in El Cerrito with Elaine.

I moved in at Elaine's sometime in 1959. I remember that Kanchan, Yasin, and Satya helped me move to Elaine's home. Elaine had given me the house key since the day we moved, and she was not going to be at her home.

It was a sad day for me to be moving away from Jerry's home. I felt horrible, especially knowing that they did not understand the reasons for my decision to move out of their home. I had gotten attached to the baby boy and the family, and leaving their home broke my heart. It was a tough time for me. Being at college was exceedingly difficult. It became apparent that now I had to compete with students who were better prepared for college than I was. In the classroom, I could see students around me in a better position to answer questions raised by the teacher. It was clear to me alone that I lacked confidence in college and felt inadequate in competing with others for better grades. I would be at a loss to answer a question when prompted to do so by the professor. It was very apparent while taking basic mathematics classes (algebra, geometry, and trigonometry). There was a lot of pressure on me to do well in college. It was because of my status of being on a student visa. I was required to maintain a GPA of C average at a minimum to remain in the US. Just the idea of being sent back home to Fiji was always an issue. Plus, I was having a tough time adjusting to all the changes happening in my life. I was still a teenager, and changing schools and living places with new people was very disruptive.

Chapter 53

ELAINE'S HOME *in* EL CERRITO

AFTER MOVING TO El Cerrito with Elaine, my life began to improve. One of the primary reasons for this was that I was already getting familiar with my surroundings. Secondly, and most importantly, Elaine was a schoolteacher and would better understand my needs. More importantly, she had friends who were schoolteachers. I remember meeting one of Elaine's closest male friends who taught at a nearby school in El Cerrito. Milton was very close to Elaine and used to visit her often. He was a constant companion to Elaine on weekends. They both were interested in supporting me with my college education program.

Milton was around Elaine a lot, and through that relationship, I was able to get needed assistance with my college courses. Milton lived alone in El Cerrito, near to Elaine, so we often saw him. He was a schoolteacher and was helpful to me, especially in English. I remember getting help from him in English Literature. He helped me get through my English 1A class, a required course for pre-med at the college.

I was fortunate enough to meet some of Elaine's other friends while staying with her. Dorothy Polara, a schoolteacher, was a perfect friend of Elaine's. She and her husband were genuinely nice to me. Dorothy was always very entertaining and often would invite us for dinner at her home in Martinez. Her husband worked at a refinery in Richmond. He also knew how to fly a small airplane. Once he took me with him to fly the plane over the Bay Area. I was scared, but after a few hours of flying, it was an excellent outing. We flew over Berkeley, Richmond, and El Cerrito, and all the Bay Area cities. My first experience on a small plane is a beautiful memory.

After flying, we had a lovely dinner at his home. Another person that used to visit Elaine regularly was Helen; she was also a schoolteacher. She liked to paint as well. Elaine and Helen had this in common. Helen often used to invite us for dinner. I enjoyed her company. She had a few of her friends, and I had an opportunity to meet them as well. There were these two young gay men that frequented Elaine's home. I was extremely comfortable with them, and they were genuinely nice to me. During those days, there was not as much talk about gay people as there is nowadays. They would also invite us to their home for dinner.

Chapter 54

CCJC *from* EL CERRITO

GOING TO EL Cerrito was tough, and I am not sure how I managed to get to school, but I did. Getting to Contra Costa Junior College from Elaine's home at El Cerrito was a real problem. I had to take three different buses. Similarly, I had to do the same coming back from school. Fortunately, I had stayed connected with Kanchan, who had a motorcycle. He knew of my situation and agreed to sell his bike to me for $125. I had to take a loan from Elaine to buy this bike. It was a good thing for me to do this since going to college was a challenge. Kanchan stayed at an airbase, and driving me to the airbase required some skill. He showed me the bike and made sure that I learned to ride it for a few minutes. After a very brief lesson, I got the bike and began a ride back to El Cerrito. In the evening, I got on the bike and biked to Elaine's home in El Cerrito. I had not been on a motorcycle before, and this was a bona fide experience. I was particularly apprehensive about going over the San Rafael Bridge. It was getting dark, there was an icy breeze, and it was a little windy; thus, crossing over the bridge at night was very scary. I did manage to make it home to El Cerrito. Elaine was very relieved to see me home safe.

At Contra Costa College, I met several international students. Many students were from South America, several from Iran, and a few from Vietnam and Thailand. The classes I took were tough. Kanti was very instrumental in helping me pick the types. As I recall, he assisted me in signing me into the pre-med program, which meant that I would be taking some tough subjects. My first semester courses were in mathematics, English, and science. I had a great deal of difficulty in English and mathematics but felt good about biological science.

My first semester in college was challenging. I was not able to make the necessary adjustment from adult high school to junior college. The competition at the junior college level was much higher than I had experienced before. It became clear that not having adequate high school foundation courses was a significant factor. As well, I did not have enough time to study. Staying with Elaine for room and board meant that I had to work for her. Weekend gardening, house cleaning, and general maintenance around the home took time away from my studies. I also needed money to buy books, pay for pocket expenses, and more.

By the second semester of being in college, I was getting used to my surroundings. It was due to becoming involved in a foreign student club. Here, I met students who were in many ways like my situation. However, many were much better off than I and came from the countries better known than Fiji. In many cases, they had better financial support and were better prepared for college than I was. One such student was Peter Chang. Peter Chang was from Vietnam. Peter lived in El Cerrito as well, not too far from where I was staying. He was living with a family similarly as I was for room and board. Both of us lived in El Cerrito, and attending the same college provided us the opportunity to help each other as needed. Having this in familiar and being international students, we became terrific friends. Peter opened my eyes to many things. One of the primary reasons for this was that Peter had come from a wealthy family in Vietnam. His father was a banker, and his family was well-to-do. I, on the other hand, came from a village life and a low-income family. We did not have access to electricity or running water. Most of our neighbors were in a comparable situation. The farmer's life was routine and predictable. Our contacts were primarily with other farmers in the village. There was minimal opportunity to meet people who were well off. Most importantly, our life was always a struggle. We relied on farming for everything, including money. However, the money earned from sugarcane just was not enough to support our large and growing family. Coming from such an environment and making the necessary adjustments to the American way of life was challenging.

Contra Costa Junior College was located in Richmond on San Pablo Avenue. It was some distance from El Cerrito. I felt truly fortunate to attend this college, since many students represented countries other than the United States of America. It was good to associate with these students and learn about their countries, but more importantly, we were all in a similar boat. All of us needed to understand the English language and be able to do well in our classes. Junior college was appropriate for me; however, I continued to struggle with my schoolwork. I found the pre-med courses challenging. Most of the students appeared better prepared for these courses than I was. I continued to have difficulties because of not having the foundation and not completing high school earlier.

Chapter 55

JUNIOR COLLEGE CHALLENGES

STARTING JUNIOR COLLEGE classes was much different from my year and a half at the adult high school. I found college classes exceedingly difficult. No matter how hard I worked in my classes, my grades continued to be C's. I remember being very discouraged, and I wanted to give up college life. But this was not possible since I was on a student visa. I remember talking with other international students, and they were experiencing similar problems. Knowing this, I felt a need to continue college life.

During the semester breaks, I would continue to work at odd jobs for Elaine's friends. I still needed to do the work for Elaine to fulfill my obligation to get room and board. Staying at Elaine's was becoming more manageable, and I could still work for some of her friends during the weekends. Elaine continued to be supportive of my needs and was extremely helpful in making sure that my studies at the college remained a priority. She was a terrific company for me. Our relationship was like mother and son. She was interested in me as a person and thought very highly of my character. I also felt good being around her and tried my best to make her life comfortable. At one time, she asked me if I wanted her to adopt me. I am not sure of the answer I gave her, but I felt uncomfortable with the question since my parents in Fiji were still alive.

Elaine had a family in British Columbia. Her sister and an aunt lived in Vancouver. Her aunt came to visit Elaine while I worked at night at Chef Boyardee after attending school all day. I would leave home from El Cerrito to work in San Leandro, the company's facility. I would start work at six in the evening and would work until two in the morning. After work, Millie, Elaine's aunt, would be waiting for me when I returned home. She made sure that I returned home safely. Millie would insist on making breakfast and make sure that I ate before going to bed. It was such a lovely thing she would do for me. Of course, the next day, I would get up by seven in the morning and get ready to go to school. A strict schedule indeed, but I had to do it. Millie was an adorable and very caring person. She would look after me like a son.

Elaine's family in Burlingame needed her house painted. Elaine volunteered me to do the painting. I remember having to stay at Mrs. Reddy's home. Mrs. Reddy was related to Elaine's husband's family. Mrs. Reddy was a wealthy woman and lived in a big home in Burlingame. It was huge, and only one person was living in the house. Mrs. Reddy did not live in the house but stayed in a cottage next to the house.

I stayed with Mrs. Reddy for a week since it took me a week to complete the paint job. In the evening, Mrs. Reddy and

I would eat dinner together. She seemed delighted to prepare the dinner and seemed to be happy with me being at her home. I felt grateful, obligated for her kindness, and wanted to pay her for expenses. She refused to take any money from me. She appreciated me for being there with her.

One incident that I will remember forever was when Mrs. Reddy had lunch at her home one weekend. There were over twenty guests and friends invited to this lunch. Elaine and I came to lunch. Elaine always liked to go and visit Mrs. Reddy. During lunch, all kinds of cold cuts were being served, along with fruit dishes and salads. I was at the head of the line, and Elaine was behind me. I took the fruit and salads as well as a few cold cuts. Elaine did not say anything while I picked on some of the cold-cut meats. Once we sat down to eat, I noticed Elaine kept looking at me as I began to eat. Once we finished eating lunch, Elaine told me that one of the cold cuts was beef tongue. I was not very happy to hear that and annoyed at Elaine for not telling me before eating that meat. I have never eaten that dish again.

Elaine, in her way, wanted me to get used to the American way of life. She and I would go for dinner occasionally, and she would introduce me to diverse types of American dishes. It was nice of her to do so for later in life. I was very thankful to her.

While staying with Elaine, my Fijian friends would visit me on a regular basis. Elaine was very fond of knowing about my friends and often would talk about how much she appreciated meeting them. However, for some reason, she did not much care for one of the boys and asked me not to invite him. I was never able to find out the reason for her feeling this way. She did not particularly like Kanti. I am not sure if there was any reason for her feeling this way. Kanti and I got along well, and he was always willing to help me with my college work. He helped me select the classes I needed to take during my first year at Contra Costa College. It might have been due to this, but I was not sure. Kanti was an excellent student attending the University of California San Francisco, in the pharmacy school. He completed his schooling and, after his graduation, went back to Fiji. The last I heard about Kanti was that Elaine met him in Canada during her visits to see her sister there. Elaine's sister had met Kanti's sister in Canada, and the two had become good friends. All went well when Elaine met Kanti's sister in Canada, and she spoke highly about them. I was delighted to hear of Elaine's change of heart about Kanti.

Chapter 56

MY SOCIAL LIFE *on* CAMPUS

IN MY SECOND year at Contra Costa Junior College, I became the president of the International Club. This club was open to all students; however, most of the members were foreigners. We met monthly on campus. There were no classes during the noon hour; thus, it was the most convenient time to meet. At the meeting, we had lots of opportunities to meet students from diverse backgrounds. Also, we had lots of opportunities to meet young ladies from various countries. I used to go on dates on a regular basis. Also, we had parties at different students' homes. Those students were often from privileged, wealthy families in their countries. By now, I was extremely comfortable being with women. I had developed a reputation around the school as an amiable and happy-go-lucky kind of guy. It was also because I owned a car, which made moving around easier. I had gotten to know a student from Thailand. He was a friendly person and always participated in foreign student activities. On a special foreign student day at campus, he used to perform for us. He demonstrated how he used to dance in Thailand. He also explained how to chew glass without causing injury to his mouth. A weird performance, but the American students enjoyed seeing his talents. After his performance, we briefly talked about how things were going for him. He was very candid about being very frustrated about being in the States. His difficulties were primarily due to not being able to communicate in English. Several other students were having similar issues. However, some could attend the technical program rather than take the regular school curriculum.

At lunch, we talked about our social issues. We had a candid chat about being frustrated with not meeting girls. He did tell me about Alexandra Mataras, a student from Greece. I am not sure how he met her, but he said to me that she lived in El Cerrito and needed a ride to get to school. He introduced me to her. Since I also lived in El Cerrito and drove to school, I promised to give her a ride to school as well. At the time, I used to date a Japanese girl, Akemi, and an Italian girl. Akemi was getting attached to me, and I was uncomfortable with this.

It was time to make a change, and I asked Alexandra for a date. Peter, my Vietnamese friend, also needed a date, and we had decided to go to see a drive-in movie in Richmond. The arrangement was that I would go with Alexandra and have Peter go with Akemi. At the last minute, Akemi did not want to go with Peter. It was too late to cancel, so when I went to pick up Alexandra, I told her of the situation. She was not happy but went along with it. So, there was me in the front seat with Akemi, and Alexandra was in the back seat with Peter. It was not a comfortable situation for either of us.

The next day I asked Alexandra to forgive me and wanted to make it up to her by going out alone. Alexandra asked me to have dinner at her brother's home where she was staying. She wanted me to meet her family before going out on a date with me again. Dimitri Mataras, her brother, and Jeannette, her Italian sister-in-law, lived in El Cerrito. I did have a wonderful dinner with her family and was happy to meet them. After getting to know the family, I was welcome to visit them anytime.

Dimitri's wife, Jeannette, visited Hawaii and was very curious about me being from the Fiji Islands. She took a particular interest in getting to know me.

One weekend, when I was painting Elaine's rental property in El Cerrito, Jeannette came to visit me. It just so happened that Elaine had come by to see my progress. She was not too happy to see Jeannette visiting me during working hours. That evening she asked me about my relationship with Jeannette. I assured her that nothing was going on between us.

Peter Chang and I used to meet regularly and talk about some of our shared challenges. He used to tell me about his work at Potluck, a restaurant in Berkeley. The restaurant was on San Pablo Avenue, not too far from Oakland. Peter was able to get me a job at the restaurant. Mr. Ed Brown was the proprietor of this restaurant. Peter spoke French and had an amicable relationship with Mr. Brown. They both would love to talk in French often. Mr. Brown loved his restaurant and was proud to serve French food. Since I had never worked at any restaurant, there was a lot for me to learn.

I started out working in the kitchen, as a dishwasher. Since I had to wash everything by hand, it was critical not to break any glasses, plates, utensils, and other fragile items. All the cooking pots and pans also had to be washed. I worked for three evenings per week. I got paid $1.25 per hour. After a month of doing this job, I was happy to get a kitchen helper job. It improved, especially since I learned how to clean and correctly set up the dinner table. Also, I was responsible for making sure that every table had white linen along with the napkin, forks, knife, and water glasses.

Peter worked as a waiter at the restaurant and was very good at it. He was always interested in me being a waiter as well. Peter used to teach me how to become a waiter while I was a kitchen helper. He was very generous with his time and taught me about the menu and serving the clientele.

It was not too long before I got promoted to a waiter at a Potluck restaurant. I was delighted to be working as a waiter. Being a waiter meant that I would serve the people who were seated at my tables. Now I had a new opportunity to impress those I did, which would translate into additional income. The money was good, and the clients liked me very much. Most of the money that we made was from tips. It meant that I no longer needed to do gardening for income, which was a good thing.

While at Potluck, I came to meet a few people and became good friends with them. Esther, an elderly black lady, was the cook. She liked me and was always willing to help me out. I remember as a waiter, she would make sure that my orders were ready very quickly. Esther helped me immensely in serving my clients rapidly, thus making the tables available for newcomers.

There at the restaurant, I had the opportunity to eat all kinds of French food. One of the most unusual dishes was frog legs, an expensive item, and we were not to eat this dish. Esther, the cook, however, insisted that I try it. She used to tell me that as a waiter, I needed to try to eat these unique dishes to explain the words to our clients better. I ate it and found it to be acceptable. Some of the other dishes that I ate were chicken liver, filet mignon, Hungarian stuffed cabbage, sweetbreads, and more. These were some new dishes that I did not get to eat when I worked at the student boarding home, where I received two meals instead of getting paid for two hours of work per evening.

The restaurant used to serve wine, and it was not difficult to get used to drinking wine with dinner. We used to eat dinner at the restaurant. It was part of our wages, though we were limited to eating only cheaper food. However, Esther would cook me any dish that I wanted. She was such a sweet lady. Esther had learned to cook all styles of French cooking. She was a lovely woman and was very fond of us. She recognized that we all were working hard to complete our education. All the waiters working at the restaurant were students, most going to the University of California. Peter and I were the only ones going to Contra Costa Junior College. Esther knew about our struggle and was always there to help us. She was one fine lady.

Chapter 57

MY SECOND YEAR *at* CCJC

MY SECOND YEAR at CCJC was not very eventful. I continued working at Potluck and also going to school. Things were getting better due to my familiarity with schooling as well as work. Elaine was accommodating in keeping me focused in school since it was straightforward to get distracted by social events. The reason is that I was still a nineteen-year-old teenager from Fiji and had not yet gotten used to the American way of life.

I had become a popular kid at Contra Costa Junior College. It was primarily due to being the president of the International Student Club on campus. We often had international events on campus, which allowed many students to participate with us.

An incident I remember well was with one of the students, who came from Cuba. He was well off and had a party at his apartment in Richmond. I went to the party without a date. At the party, there were several students from South America. We were having a fun time, and I began to enjoy the company of this one young lady. She liked me, and I was interested in her as well. Before I knew it, the woman's boyfriend became very upset with me because, as he stated, I was stealing his girlfriend. Of course, I did not have any intention of stealing anyone's girlfriend. When I told Elaine of this incident, she started to laugh. I did not understand the meaning of this. Elaine said that this was very common in America and that I needed to be aware of girls who may be attracted to me and were willing to dump their boyfriends for me. Wow! Elaine told me to watch out for girls because I was a handsome young man. Additionally, being from Fiji appeared to be an attraction in and of itself.

I continued to see Alexandra, and we became very close. Our relationship went beyond just being friends. It was not uncommon for us to go out on dates after my shifts at the restaurant ended. Peter, Alexandra, and I would often go out for Chinese food. Our favorite location was Chinatown. We would pick up Alexandra after work from El Cerrito and go to Oakland Chinatown for Chinese food. The three of us also traveled to Yosemite National Park. It was an impromptu decision, so we picked up Alexandra after work and drove most of the night to reach the park. After a few hours at the park, we came back to our home.

I began to see Alexandra often both at school and after work hours. We became close and talked about getting married. Alexandra was interested but wanted me to speak with her brother before she would agree. Since I had gotten to know her brother well, I did not see any problem asking Dimitris about my plan. I think it had become clear to both Dimitris and his wife that we were obviously in love, and they both consented for us to get married. I also talked with Elaine about my plan, and she did not object. However, she was very concerned about us still being in school and being on student visas. Simply put, she was very supportive and wished us the best of luck.

Chapter 58

A SIMPLE WEDDING

WE SET DECEMBER 17, 1960, as our marriage date. We faced a few challenges, such as being from different religions. Alexandra is a Greek Orthodox Christian, and I am a Hindu, which meant that we could not be married in the Greek Orthodox Church. So the next best thing was to get married in a civil court, which we did. Dimitris and Jeannette had an excellent reception for us at their home. A few of our best friends were in attendance at our wedding. Peter was my best man, and Alexandra had a young lady from Colombia, South America, as her bridesmaid. After our marriage, we stayed at Elaine's home for a few weeks. Elaine, as always, was very aware of our situation in that we could not go away for a few days for our honeymoon. So, she decided to spend the weekend in Burlingame so we could be at her home alone.

After her return from Burlingame, we talked about finding a place to stay. We decided to look for an apartment, but where? Since I still worked at the Potluck restaurant, we decided to find a place in Berkeley. We did finally find a place on Blake Street in Berkeley. The apartment was in the back of a two-story building. A schoolteacher was renting the upstairs of the building; we rented the lower unit. It was a small place but comfortable for the two of us. Most important for us was the cost issue since both of us had to continue going to school. Being on student visas, we could work only on a part-time basis.

Chapter 59

OUR FIRST DAUGHTER *is* BORN

THOSE DAYS WERE not only challenging but also happy ones, since now we expected a child. Beverly, our first child, was born in June 1961. She was born at Herrick Memorial Hospital. Fortunately for us, the hospital was close to our apartment. Both the mother and baby were healthy and doing well and were discharged from the hospital after three days. It was good to have them home, and since we were off school, this allowed a few months of precious time for Alexandra to stay with our baby. Also, we had time to begin planning for the fall semester, which meant that we would need to find someone to look after our baby while we continued to attend school. There was this lady next door who showed interest in taking care of our child. We both felt comfortable with her and decided she could look after our daughter while we went to school. Beverly was only three months old at the time. It was tough to leave our baby with a babysitter at such a tender age, but we had little choice in the matter. After school, we would rush back home to see our little one.

Alexandra graduated from Contra Costa College with her AA degree, while I still had a few more semesters to go. It was because I was in a pre-med program. Money was always an issue with us, and especially now, we had added expenses. My wife found a job at a local restaurant and began to work. She primarily worked on weekends while I looked after our daughter Beverly. I continued to go to school and work at Potluck during the evening shift. Our life together became even more challenging with having a child. However, it was a wonderful moment, which made us more determined to succeed in life.

Chapter 60

MY THIRD YEAR *at* CCJC

FINALLY, I WAS able to meet all the requirements to graduate from Contra Costa Junior College. During my last semester of school, I repeated a second-semester zoology course. There was a minimal choice in selecting the teachers for the zoology classes. Dr. Tarp taught this class. He was very proud of having graduated from Stanford University. All the students taking his class felt intimidated by his teaching technique; in other words, he was a very demanding professor. He had very high standards and was a harsh grader.

I continued to have difficulty with this class and needed to get a C grade to graduate. I did not get a C and thus most likely would not be accepted at San Francisco State University. I had to consult with him about what my next step would be. After a brief discussion, he was willing to review my status, especially when I made him aware of some of the pre-med students in his class who already had BA degrees. He was not aware of this. What had happened to this class was that around five students were taking the same courses as I was. These students already had graduated from college with BA degrees and were repeating all the pre-med courses. They were interested in attending medical school, and therefore were retaking their zoology class with Dr. Tarp. It seemed very unfair, but that was the way it was. So asking him to reconsider changing my grade from a D to a C was not in any way promoting favoritism.

My wife had already graduated from this college a year earlier. It was extremely critical that I also earn my AA degree. I managed to graduate in June 1962. I felt such a feeling of accomplishment. I was a kid from Fiji who had come to the United States without any high school education, and I was receiving a diploma. It felt terrific that I could get this, the very first academic degree in my life. It was a significant achievement for me since I did not have a high school diploma. Also, it was the very first time that I felt it would be possible for me to excel in academia. With that in mind, I applied to San Francisco State University. Fortunately for me, I was accepted to this college in 1962. Of course, now we faced another challenge: We would need to move to San Francisco from Berkeley. The idea of moving away from family and friends was of concern, especially since we had little knowledge of the new location.

PART XIII:

RELOCATING *to* SAN FRANCISCO

Chapter 61

OUR APARTMENT *in* HAIGHT-ASHBURY

ALEXANDRA AND I lived in El Cerrito when I was accepted SFSU, so we needed to move to San Francisco. It was challenging to relocate, but we were delighted to start a new life across the Bay. We lived on the second floor of the building, our first apartment on Waller Street in Haight-Ashbury. The apartment was old but acceptable for the student lifestyle. Alexandra and I always considered our daughter Beverly's schooling and babysitting issues. It was always our primary concern. My wife had located a school around North Beach in San Francisco for Beverly to attend. The school was under control and operated by nuns, which assured us of safety and security for our young child. These nuns were extremely strict but looked after our daughter with care and fondness.

Chapter 62

SAN FRANCISCO STATE UNIVERSITY

I STARTED SAN Francisco State University in the spring of 1963. San Francisco State University remains at 1600 Holloway Drive. It was some distance from our apartment but was still easily accessible. I felt good about my first semester. More importantly, there was such pride in being at the university. Now I had an opportunity to obtain an undergraduate degree. I was in the biological sciences department with an initial emphasis on botany. Nine units out of the twelve that I was taking were about the plant kingdom. I found the professors to be outstanding in their fields. Dr. Sweeney was interested in taking field trips and was highly interested in plants that survived under adverse conditions. Dr. Thiers was interested in mycology and always asked his students to look for mushrooms.

I remember going to Golden Gate Park with my daughter Beverly when she was five years old to look for mushrooms. I showed her how to collect the fungi and how to preserve them. She seemed happy to learn the names of these plants, and wherever we visited, she would tell people of our venture in the park and about the fungi. Many people were amazed to see that this little kid knew about fungi. Elaine Levesque used to get a kick out of Beverly's curiosity surrounding fungi, and it became routine for her to mention it to all her friends.

I continued to have difficulties with my coursework. It was very frustrating that I could not get better grades. I worked extremely hard to keep a B average, but it did not happen. Courses in Medical Microbiology and Genetics just did not agree with me. Now I was studying on a full-time basis. It was because my wife began to work full-time at the Red Cross. I only worked during the summer months.

I was truly fortunate to find a job at Chef Boyardee in San Leandro. Mr. Basil Rao and some of his family members worked there, and I found the summer job attractive. My job was to provide the cook with a concrete mix of spices for the spaghetti sauce. The work itself was not difficult. However, the hours were hard since I worked on the night shift.

Before working at Chef Boyardee, I worked on an assembly line at American Motors. I was responsible for putting on the bumper on the trucks. It was the most challenging work I had ever done, and the workers were awfully hard on me. They had no mercy and used foul language, especially when I could not complete putting on the fifteen bolts on the assembly line required to secure the bumper. After two weeks at this job, I could not continue and quit; luckily, Mr. Basil Rao could hire me at Chef Boyardee. The experience of working at American Motors is something that I will never forget. It is because of the type of workers that were there. These workers were there to get a paycheck, and a childish-looking college kid was not going to get in their way.

Chapter 63

STUDENT HOUSING

DURING MY SECOND year, we were able to move into a student housing building run by SFSU. This place used to be old army housing units and had gotten converted to student housing. It was not the best facility, but given our situation, it worked well. The rent was $45 per month, and that was simply fine. Most importantly, the school was close by, and it was perfect for me since it allowed me to focus entirely on my studies. The housing was also close to Stonestown Shopping Center. My wife worked full-time at the Red Cross, and it was easier for her to take the train. She used to take Beverly on the train to her school near the Broadway Entertainment Center. It was a long way from our home, and traveling was difficult and time-consuming, but she did this the entire time while I was at San Francisco State University. She took the train from Stonestown and transferred to a bus to take Bev to her school at North Beach. After dropping Bev at school, she would take another bus to work at the Red Cross on Sutter Street. She also had to pick up Bev from the school in the evening to come home. Life was tough for my wife while I was doing my full-time studies at the university, but she never complained. I, however, continued to struggle at the university. My grades just would not go over a B average, no matter how hard I tried. Although it was very frustrating, I kept plugging away. At school, I met many good people, including professors. We had some good days, but overall, things were challenging. We did not get any support from anyone, and getting a loan while on a student visa was impossible.

During my second year at San Francisco State, my brother Bhupendra Kumar arrived from Fiji to do his studies. My brother Ramesh, who I had assisted in getting to the States for his studies, was most helpful in getting Bhupendra to come to the States. Ramesh had helped him come to the States on a student visa, and he was to attend the College of San Mateo. Ramesh was already at the College of San Mateo and knew his way around, but I was unsure where Bhupendra would stay. While we needed to work out this minor detail, Bhupendra stayed with us at our student housing. It was difficult for three adults and a child to remain in a tiny apartment, but we managed. Bhupendra stayed with us for a few weeks only and later went to live with Ramesh. It was Ramesh who helped Bhupendra to come to the States with the help of Mrs. Sue Smith. Mrs. Smith at the time lived in San Carlos, California. Ramesh was fortunate to find such a lovely family and seemed happy to have her support.

Chapter 64

SUMMER JOBS

WHILE GOING TO SFSU, I was fortunate to work at American Home Foods in San Leandro. I was also able to continue working at Elaine's house and helped her with her gardening needs and house duties as needed. We often visited her, and she kept encouraging me to continue with my studies. Elaine had become remarkably close to us and wanted us to succeed. She knew our situation the best and helped us with groceries. We spent most of the holidays with Elaine in El Cerrito. We also had to spend a few holidays with Jeannette's family in Livermore. There were many happy days, especially the Christmas holidays, an important holiday for us. I remember driving to Livermore, where Natalie, one of Jeannette's daughters, and Manos, Natalie's husband, lived. It was one of those days where the fog covered the valley. Driving back home was tough, but we made it home safely. Christmas holidays were particularly challenging for us. Elaine always expected us to be with her during this holiday. When we could not make this happen, she would get agitated and let us know her feelings.

For me, it was not important where we would spend Christmas, but this was important to my wife. She wanted to spend more time with her side of the family. Dimitris, her brother, did not have much choice as his wife preferred being around her family. Even though a major issue every year for us, it was good to know that friends and family members cared enough wanting us to be with them.

Chapter 65

GRADUATION

AFTER TWO YEARS, I was finally able to complete the required courses to receive an undergraduate degree in biology. It was one of the happiest days of my life. The struggle and challenges were all worth the effort. I am sure those close to me also felt relief that now I could work and earn a decent living. As I recall, I was not able to participate in the graduation ceremony to receive my diploma. The biggest reason was that I lacked the money to purchase a cap and gown. Not being able to participate in the graduation ceremony was a significant disappointment. I remember some of my friends asked if I would be with them, but I made some excuse that I had to work or something. Of course, now I had an opportunity to work and make a living to support my family. It was not so, however, since a degree in biology could not open doors for me. Therefore, I decided to go to summer school to get a master's degree. I signed up for a course in physiology, which was a tough challenge since I had to attend the lecture on three separate days and be in the lab for two hours once a week. It was not a smart move since I had to work at Chef Boyardee in San Leandro from six in the evening to two in the morning. Earning income in the summer months was essential, and attempting to take a five-unit course at the same time was exceedingly difficult. One thing that turned out well was that I met a student who was in a similar predicament. This person, a Greek man, worked full time at the San Quentin Jail as a medical technologist and took the physiology course with me. We became good friends, but schooling was difficult for both of us.

One of the most important things was that he showed me a flyer on the bulletin board. This flyer asked biology students to apply for training in medical technology at either Kaiser in San Francisco or Stanford University in Palo Alto. I was very excited about the possibility of being at a hospital to do an internship in the medical technology program. The program would pay a stipend for the year, and after a year, I would be allowed to sit for a licensing exam. Since I did not have many options, I completed the necessary papers and submitted my application to both training schools. I was pleasantly surprised to hear that both training programs offered me a position. I decided to go to Kaiser Foundation Hospital. I was delighted and saw a window of opportunity for my future. Stanford was quite far from our apartment, and they were paying only a $100 per month stipend, while Kaiser in San Francisco was paying a salary of $250 per month and, more importantly, was walking distance from our apartment.

At the time, we lived on Sixth Avenue in the Richmond District. We had to move out of the student housing after my graduation and had to find an apartment. It was decent-sized and had a backyard. Also, we wanted to make sure that our daughter Beverly could go to school nearby. Moving back to San Francisco was also suitable for my wife because it aided her commute to work. All in all, things had started to work out for us.

PART XIV:

KAISER FOUNDATION HOSPITAL

Chapter 66

INTERNSHIP *at* KAISER HOSPITAL *in* SAN FRANCISCO

KAISER HOSPITAL IS in San Francisco on Geary Street. The location is next to the old Sears Robuck store. It is one of the larger hospitals in the Kaiser system. Once I started the program, it became abundantly clear that I had made the right decision. Dr. Milton Basis was the Director of Pathology, and Mrs. Weber was both the Teaching Coordinator and the Assistant Chief of the Clinical Laboratory. Dr. Betty Thomas was chief pathologist of the Clinical Laboratory. Miss Zamet was the Chief of the Clinical Laboratory. I was among five students selected for the training program, and I was the only man in the group. There were not too many male students interested in the medical technology field during this time.

Our phlebotomy teacher was Gladys, a registered nurse. One of the duties for us was to make our phlebotomy rounds with qualified medical technologists. Before starting this program, Gladys would gather us and go over the technique and the principle behind drawing blood. Gladys was one of the best teachers of phlebotomy. She always referred to the group as "ladies," and I had to remind her that I was a man and did not wish to be called a lady.

Chapter 67

STUDENTS' ROTATION THROUGH ALL *the* LABORATORY DEPARTMENTS

THE ORGANIZATION OF the Clinical Laboratory at Kaiser Foundation Hospital in San Francisco into various departments is for an efficient system. The significant departments were Chemistry, Special Chemistry, Hematology, Serology, Microbiology, and Transfusion Services. There was also the Anatomical Pathology department. The Anatomical Pathology department had two major divisions: the Cytology department, which was away from the hospital, and the Histology department, located on the second floor of the hospital. We had to rotate through all these departments and sit through one hour of lectures every day for five days each week.

In each department, we had to learn the principles of the test and the technology used. In 1966, the Clinical Laboratory purchased some automated equipment such as the Single Channel Autoanalyzer by Technicon, semi-automated analyzers in the Hematology department, and other types of technology needed to get the required test done. I think every clinical laboratory throughout the country was similarly equipped. My rotation started in Clinical Chemistry. The department had up to five technologists. The lead technologist took responsibility for the student for the chemistry section. My instructor's name was Clarence Thomas, and he was the only male in the department and, in fact, the only male throughout the laboratory. He had a good reputation for being very tough on the new students. I found him to be very knowledgeable. He was very dedicated to his profession, and therefore my first rotation was very inspiring. After the Chemistry rotation, I got assigned to Hematology. This section had two technologists who were both Filipinos.

One of the technologists was amazing, especially at the manual differential. This unique procedure requires making a smear of whole blood on a glass slide. Once the smear slide is dry, it is then stained to differentiate the various cell types, then examined under a microscope. While the technologist reviews the slide under the microscope, she can count the several types of cells that she sees. She would count to one hundred cells, and that number was recorded, which became part of the CBC or complete blood cell count. It was not an easy task, and for me, to see how quickly she performed it was amazing. I swear that she felt comfortable that doing differentials was quite easy and that over ninety percent of the time, the microscopic testing would be in the normal range. This procedure was in the hands of individual technologists, which made it difficult to detect mistakes that may have occurred. The Hematology department was not easy to get through. The instrument was available to perform complete blood cell counts (white blood cells, red blood cells, and platelets). It was easy to perform testing on the instrument. However, I found difficulty in doing the differential, especially in identifying various abnormal cells on the slide under the microscope. It was easy to identify the red cells, white cells, and platelets, especially those within normal.

We also performed testing for hemoglobin and hematocrit. The technologist conducts the tests manually. A technologist must aspirate some whole blood into a capillary tube and then spin this into a centrifuge at around five thousand RPM. After turning for a minute, they would measure the capillary tube where the whole blood gets separated from the plasma. On the other hand, hemoglobin is measured by using a photoelectric calorimeter against a standard solution. Manual methods are simply for procedures that do not require much technology. The significant difference between chemistry testing and hematology was the type of blood sample that we used. Chemistry required a clotted blood sample, which meant that we needed to take blood from patients whose blood tubes did not have anticoagulants. This tube of clotted blood, when centrifuged, would be able to separate the red cells from the serum. Almost all tests performed in chemistry use the serum portion of the blood. On the other hand, we needed whole blood for hematology, which meant an anticoagulant in the blood tube inhibited the blood from clotting.

After hematology, my next assignment led me to the Transfusion Service. This department requires quick thinking on your feet because blood transfusion is, in most cases, an emergency procedure. Those needing blood, especially during accidents, need blood transfusions to save their lives. Also, patients going to surgery have blood ready in case of excessive bleeding. Women during childbirth may need blood transfusions as well. I found this department to be a real challenge for me, although it was a rewarding experience because of the life and death nature of the situations.

We usually needed to carry up to ninety units of blood per twenty-four-hour shift. Most of the blood unit was O-positive because up to thirty-seven percent of us have this blood type. Our blood supplier was the Erwin Memorial Blood Center in San Francisco. We carried other blood products, such as platelets, blood plasma, cryoprecipitate, and more. Human blood is very precious, and it is vital to have a unique refrigeration system for storing it properly. Thus, we needed to monitor the blood bank refrigerator temperature regularly. It was also critical that we kept a good record of temperature monitoring. It was important to maintain the refrigeration temperature between three degrees and six degrees centigrade. When there was a need for blood, patient identification was necessary. We had to do the compatibility testing of the patient receiving the blood unit and accurately identify the donor blood. The training for students in the blood bank was the most rigorous, and we were required to be very alert to make sure that we learned as much as possible.

My third rotation was in the Microbiology department. This department was very complex. I knew about bacteriology but did not focus much on parasitology, mycology, or virology. There was a significant emphasis on bacteriology, however. At the time of my rotation in this department, there was hardly any automation; therefore, a very rigorous effort was needed to use one's intellect and total focus in making the diagnoses. We had to know which specimen was required to grow the bacteria for each sample we received in the department. The technologists within the department had to have detailed knowledge on which media were compatible with which type of organism could be within the specimen. The specimen included bodily waste products such as urine, stool samples, sputum, bodily fluids, spinal fluids, and more. The rotation required was the longest in this department than any other within the Clinical Laboratory.

The final rotation was through the Histology and Cytology departments. This rotation was very unusual since it was not part of the Clinical Laboratory. However, the department directors felt that students needed to have experience in histopathology because the state would test our knowledge in this department. I enjoyed this one week in the department and found it to be fascinating.

Chapter 68

PREPARATION *for the* LICENSING EXAM

AFTER COMPLETING THE one-year training at Kaiser Foundation Hospital, we had a few weeks to prepare for our exam. The California licensing exam was comprehensive and required a passing grade of seventy percent or greater. I remember studying with my fellow students at my home. There was a consensus that we would review together and help each other to secure a license. However, no one offered to have study sessions at their home or apartment to get together for our studies.

We had to take our licensing exam in Berkeley. It was a nerve-racking day, but we were confident that we would do well because of our Kaiser training. I found the questions tricky, and I made sure that I correctly addressed all the questions. Most of the questions were from chemistry and hematology. There were a few questions from California's state law. The questions on California law required only one choice, although I answered more than one in some cases. I was genuinely concerned about this because we all were required to pass this section to be a candidate for the license. In the following week, we all needed to take the national licensing exam. This exam was for an MT license, supported by the American Society of Clinical Pathologists (MT, ASCP). This license was not required for us to practice Medical Technology in California, however.

The results came in the mail, and I discovered that I passed both the California and national program examinations and received the appropriate license. Now I could use BA, CLS, MT (ASCP) after my name. BA is a Bachelor of Arts, CLS is Clinical Laboratory Scientist in California, and MT is Medical Technologist for the national license. Indeed, it was an enormously proud moment for me. Once I had my California license and the national certification plus assurance of a job, my wife, daughter, and I decided to visit my family in Fiji.

PART XV:

RETURN *to* FIJI AFTER TEN YEARS *in the* USA

Chapter 69

GOING HOME *to* FIJI

WE MADE ALL the necessary preparation for us to take a vacation to Fiji. I was very excited and looked forward to getting reacquainted with my family and friends back home. I was returning to Fiji after ten years in America. It was exciting and somewhat sad to realize that I had changed in many ways. I was returning with a university degree and with my wife and a child. I did not pay much attention to where to stay in Fiji once we arrived; therefore, I did not make hotel arrangements. I just assumed that we would be able to stay at my mother's home. This home did not have a shower, toilet, and some of the other comforts we were used to in America. All I knew was that we would be greeted like royalty, as were my other brothers who had returned after their graduations. As one can imagine, ten years is a long time.

All things were ready for us to go. It was our most extended trip as a family, and the flight from San Francisco to Los Angeles was uneventful. After arriving in Los Angeles, we had to find a way to the International Airport, which was not easy to locate. However, we eventually found the International Airport and the location to the boarding area of Qantas Airline. Qantas was the airline that flew to Fiji during those years. Qantas Airline, at the time, was regarded as one of the better airlines. As I recall, I still had my Fijian passport, and my wife had her Greek passport, while our daughter Beverly carried her American passport. The immigration people found this remarkably interesting: three family members traveling together with three different sets of documents.

Once we boarded the plane, it was nice to be seated and ready to fly. We arrived in Honolulu after almost six hours of flying. The plane landed in Hawaii in the morning, and after a few hours, we were off to the Fiji Islands. After five hours of flight, we finally arrived at Nadi Airport. I was very relieved when the plane landed as it was getting dark. There was a massive crowd at the airport as most of my family was there to greet us. After ten years of being away from them, seeing my parents and loved ones was a very emotional moment. My first impression of seeing my family was surprising. They appeared darker in their appearance than when I had left them. They also looked older than I had expected. Not seeing my family members when over ten years had elapsed had a lot to do with the changes. Also, my being in America with Western people had a lot to do with my initial reaction.

My wife and child looked at me with surprise, but they were delighted to meet my family finally. My mother was the first one who I embraced, followed by my stepmom and my dad.

Then came my brothers and close relatives. My Brother Deo Narayan had a little car that we drove into my village. On the way to Nawaka, the road looked narrow and small. It was the opposite of when I first arrived in America. Now the reverse was true. When we arrived at my mother's home, more people were waiting to greet us. There were local Fijians with whom I played while growing up in Fiji.

My wife and daughter stayed in the house while I was with the men outside under a bright moon. I had taken with me some American tobacco and cigars. The cigars had a wooden stick at the end. It became the talk of those who smoked tobacco. It was simply something that no one had seen before. There was much excitement about the appearance of this cigar.

The family had prepared meals for us, which were difficult for my wife and child to eat since they were on the spicy side. However, there was a lot of excitement, and all were happy to see us. During the night, we slept at my mom's home. It was tough for us to adjust to what we had been used to while at home in the States. Everything around us looked small. My brother had built an English-style toilet facility for us. It was genuinely nice for him to do. It was clear that Brother Deo and the family made the extra effort to ensure that we would be comfortable staying at his home. However, things were challenging for my wife and daughter since they had to see much of the night creatures. The nightcrawlers, lizards, and cockroaches were all around us, which created lots of hardship for my wife and daughter. Also, there was a lot of noise due to the strong wind that night. The other noises made by the animals that were around the home kept us awake all night. It was challenging for us to adjust to this unfamiliar environment. None of us could sleep because of the howling wind all night long.

Morning arrived, and we were up early. My sister-in-law had already prepared tea and a breakfast of roti and curry. We were starving. I looked at my wife and knew that changes needed to occur, for we would not be able to spend another night as before. So, I brought up the subject to my brother and mother about our situation. They agreed to move up to my Brother Prem's home, which was up on the hill and modern and was where my father and his family also lived. It was much more comfortable; however, instead of a toilet, they had an outhouse. That meant that we had to go to my mother's home to use the comfort facility. My Brother Prem had fenced his property with barbed wire, making it difficult to go down the hill. There were also animals in the way, such as horses and bulls. We had to use the main road to get to my mom's home, which meant that those village people could see us going back and forth to use the comfort facilities. This arrangement worked out but created some discomfort for my wife. My daughter Beverly loved the idea since it meant that she could stop by at my brother's store to get free candy.

My dad loved Beverly very much, even though they were not able to speak with each other. You see, my father only spoke Hindi, and Beverly only spoke English, so they used their version of sign language to overcome the language barrier. He used to give her some extra coins, which she used to pay for her candies. Of course, my brother would not accept her money, and she could not understand the reason for this.

Every day was a busy day for us in Nawaka Village. The local village people would quickly visit to see us without any forewarning. Prem Narayan became our constant companion, and since he had a car, he was able to drive us around. My mother would come up to Prem's home to see us every morning. She also encouraged her elderly friends to visit us as well. Many came to see me for they had found out that I was working in the hospital and therefore knew about medicine. We also had many dinner engagement requests but had to be selective in accepting since there was not much time. More importantly, it was difficult for my wife to adjust to eating Indian food regularly. I remember accepting an invitation to have dinner at my Brother Deo Narayan's former boss's home. He was well regarded in Nadi Town and had his business for many years.

Most importantly, my brother had worked for this company for several years. Samji and Company, where my brother had worked, had become a significant part of our lives. My brother was the primary provider of consumable goods for our family. Most of the consumable items we used at home came from Samji's shop. At Samji's shop, my brother earned the utmost respect, and more importantly, he was able to get special recognition from the company frequently.

I remember while growing up that my brother would bring Samji's truck with sacks of flour, onions, garlic, tea, salt, sugar, and other smaller items every month. Neither I nor anyone else knew all that was needed, but Brother Deo Narayan did. Because he provided many of the necessary household items, our family survived without much hardship.

It should be evident that it was essential for us to accept this invitation. It was the first time I had visited Mr. Samji's home for dinner. Of course, their family treated us with the utmost respect, and the best food was made available for us. Not only did we have a delicious meal, but we were treated with gifts as well. My wife received an Indian sari and some jewelry, while my present provided a letter opener that we still use today. Beverly received some jewelry as well. All in all, we were treated with kindness and respect.

After our first week in the Nawaka village, we traveled to Suva. My Brother Prem drove us, and along the way, we stopped at some of the tourist hotels. These hotels were, in most cases, located near the beachfront. Fiji never looked better to me. You see, when I was growing up in Fiji, we were never able to see these lovely places. We could not even go near these hotels for fear of being chased away. I was a farmer, and farmers did not get much respect. So, there I was, with my wife of European descent and an American daughter who could visit places as we pleased. Along the way to Suva, the capital of Fiji, I had to acknowledge that this was the third time I was seeing this city. The first time was to attend a wedding, and the second time was to get my papers to leave Fiji for the States.

We arrived in Suva in the late afternoon. My Brother Jai and his wife Irene welcomed us to their home. Bhabhi Irene was in the Fiji Parliament and had a hectic life. She was very gracious, however, and hospitable toward my family. Their four children—Pardeep, Hermant, Renu, and Perwez—were beside themselves. Beverly enjoyed their company. Brother Jai's compound had a few coconut trees, and the boys were able to treat us with the milk and meat from the coconuts. It was the very first time Beverly and my wife ever had such a lovely treat.

In the evening, we were able to meet up with a few relatives who lived around Suva. One evening Bhabhi arranged a dinner party to meet most of our close relatives whom I had not seen for somewhere between ten to fifteen years. It was great seeing family and friends for old times' sake.

Before the evening was over, we exchanged contact information for more dinner invitations. My cousin, Chandar Shan, who lived near the Suva courthouse, was interested in showing us the city of Suva and took us for dinner at his home. It was good for me to get acquainted with him and meet his wife as well.

We had dinner invitations at Vishnu and Nirmala's home. My Brother Prem, our driver, stayed at Vishnu's home while we stayed at Brother Jai's home. Here again, Bhabhi Irene and Jai did not attend. We also were later invited for dinner at Aruna's home. All was excellent.

After a week of staying in Suva, we returned to Nawaka and stayed at Prem's home. By that time, we were ready to leave Fiji. That evening, there was a family gathering to say goodbye to us. Frankly, we were somewhat anxious to return to the States. One of the primary reasons was to start work at the Kaiser Foundation Hospital, where I had completed my training.

We returned home safely and had to vacate the housing from the San Francisco State College housing complex. We moved to 18th Avenue in the Sunset District. It was close to my work and convenient for Beverly's school.

Chapter 70

PAPU COMES TO AMERICA

IN 1968, MY wife's father, Mr. Nicholas Mataras, came to the States at around this time. Dimitris Mataras, his son, wanted to help his family in Greece. Like other children from Europe and other countries, all they wanted to do was the best for their parents and family. He was fortunate to have his father migrate from Greece.

I remember when he landed at San Francisco Airport. There was a lot of excitement, and my wife and family were thrilled to see him. Since Dimitris lived in Livermore, my father-in-law went to live with Dimitris and Jeannette, his wife. Jeannette had some difficulties adjusting to living with an older Greek man; however, things worked until my father-in-law's son Paul arrived in 1969. When Paul Mataras, Alexandra's half-brother, arrived, he stayed with us for a while. I was able to help him get a job at San Francisco's Kaiser Hospital as well. Mr. Mataras and his son moved in together in Berkeley. Mr. Mataras was able to get a job in Berkeley as a dishwasher. It was hard on my father-in-law. It was also hard for me to see him do this type of work at his age. Being an immensely proud and independent man, he wanted to make a living on his terms. Just imagine: Mr. Mataras had survived the Second World War and raised his family in Greece at that tough time. Thus, it did not matter the kind of job he had if it was honest. I felt sad for him, but we did not have much choice since the poor man needed to help pay for his rent. We were just starting in life and could not help to support him and Paul. My wife and I had truly little to offer. I had spent a good ten years completing my education. I was fortunate enough to meet the internship at the Kaiser Foundation Hospital and incredibly lucky to start working there afterward. At the time, my income was about $10 per hour.

Paul Mataras did well at Kaiser and learned about computer systems. Paul was a brilliant boy and quickly realized his capacity for working with computers. At this time, the hospital had ventured into computerizing the laboratory. Paul became an asset in running the day-to-day computer system. It was challenging since the IBM computer system was based on a card system. Looking back, it was a disaster, but Paul and Bob Hass kept us going under the direction of Dr. Betty Thomas.

Alexandra's sister, Marika, arrived in America on March 14, 1970. She stayed with us at 20 Nelson Court in Daly City. She later decided to go to Livermore and work with her brother Dimitris. At the time, Dimitris owned a deli shop where Marika would work along with Jeannette. It turned out to be a disaster since Marika and Jeannette did not see eye-to-eye. We then had to have her come back to our home at Nelson Court and stay with us. After a week of staying at home with us, I was able to get her a job at Kaiser Hospital Laboratory. We always needed phlebotomists in the laboratory, and I felt Marika would learn this rather quickly.

Marika was a beautiful young lady and had no problem getting recognized by her coworkers. All the men, who were few, were interested in getting to know her. But she did not know how to adjust from Greece to America. She was a quick learner, and the phlebotomy technique and patient care came easy for her. All those that came to know her were extremely impressed with her performance. She received much support from the laboratory's leadership since they knew about our relationship. She also received a lot of guidance from my wife since she had had similar experiences when she first arrived in this country.

Soon after, Mrs. Mataras, Alexandra's stepmother, arrived in the USA. The family was able to move back to San Francisco and live as a family unit. It was not to last very long as Marika decided to move into her apartment near her place of employment.

Chapter 71

FIRST FULL-TIME JOB *as a* MEDICAL TECHNOLOGIST

MY FIRST DAY of work at Kaiser Foundation Hospital Laboratory in San Francisco was in the Hematology department. The two ladies who worked in this department were very efficient and highly productive, making it a challenge to keep up with them. More importantly, there was just enough work for two technologists. So, I was assigned to the Chemistry department. I learned very quickly and became efficient with the Clinical Laboratory instrumentation. There was also a special chemistry section where we performed thyroid function tests. I got to be particularly good in this department and ended up there for almost six months. My next rotation was in Microbiology and Transfusion Services. It was orientation, and thus I did not get to stay in the department for longer than necessary. I found the rotation through all the departments to be immensely helpful as well as a confidence builder. Thus, I was now ready to be on call. Being on call meant that if staffing became overwhelmed with the workload, the person on call got to come and help as needed. I was ready to make extra money outside of my regular schedule to position myself for additional income. It had become apparent that my wife and I needed to save money to buy a house.

I decided to work part-time, just twenty hours per week, at French Hospital. I was offered a position after all the training and rotations through the different departments. I worked mainly in the evenings and on weekends. After six months of working part-time at French Hospital, I realized that I could work an additional eight hours at Kaiser and that it would be much better if I did so. I began to work at Kaiser on Friday nights. It was possible since after working five days per week during the day shift, I could then work eight hours of the graveyard shift and get paid for twelve hours of overtime. It worked out well for the time being, and we had saved almost enough money to put a down payment for our new home in Daly City. Our daughter, Beverly, was having a hard time in the San Francisco school system, so this idea of moving away from the city was good for the family. We still did not have enough money for the down payment, however. We needed an additional thousand dollars. We asked Peter Shankar's mother for a loan, and she kindly gave us the money at five percent interest. With this money, we were able to buy our first home in Daly City.

I continued learning about medicine in the Clinical Laboratory and began to take more classes at San Francisco State University. It was the best thing for my future, as learning both the principles and technological bases of a chemistry procedure allowed me to become the supervisor of the Chemistry department. It was an achievement for me since several people were better qualified for the position. Additionally, they were at the laboratory much longer than I. Only two years after working in the laboratory, I got promoted to a management position. Dr. Betty Thomas, a very bright clinical pathologist, quizzed me constantly on various aspects of chemistry and other departments within the Clinical Laboratory. She was astute and made sure that all the department heads had a good grasp of clinical pathology. She was always after me to take classes and become the best that I could be.

At the time, Kaiser had started to multiply, and San Francisco Kaiser began to take the lead among other Kaiser hospitals. It was due to Dr. Milton Basis and Dr. Betty Thomas. These two were the best pathologists within the Kaiser system at the time. To the best of my recollection, Dr. Thomas was the only clinical pathologist within the Kaiser system. Dr. Basis was one of the best anatomical pathologists. He used to have more than three to four resident pathologists in any given year. Thus, Dr. Basis received much recognition from other Kaiser hospitals.

By now, I began to manage the whole Clinical and Anatomical Laboratory departments. I was promoted to assistant chief technologist, replacing Mrs. Yoshi Weber. Mrs. Weber became a full-time teaching coordinator. At this time, we began to train around twelve medical technology students. Miss Zermatt remained as chief technologist. She started to report directly to Mr. Deveron. Mr. Deveron became the manager of the laboratory. It was a new title created for the San Francisco Kaiser Hospital Laboratory. Mr. Deveron was not a licensed technologist, so I am not sure why he got this position. At the time, it became clear that there were many things behind the scenes that were happening.

There were three facets of politics going on. First was Dr. Basis, who was the director of the laboratory. There was Dr. Thomas, who was the clinical pathologist. Finally, there was the administration. I tried hard not to get involved in many of these issues and concerns. However, it was clear that Kaiser was becoming the largest health maintenance organization (HMO) in the United States. The Kaiser Foundation Hospital managed the health plan, and there was the Permanente Medical Group. The Permanente Medical Group was composed of all physicians organized to deliver medical care for the members. One had to be a member of the Kaiser Health Plan to receive care from the physician group. So, I worked for the Permanente Medical Group rather than the Kaiser Health Plan.

While many political games were happening around me, I focused on continuing education and taking classes in management and laboratory fields. It became apparent that I had to be good at leadership and a sound laboratory scientist to be a better leader. It was not long before I began to take symposiums from different manufacturers of laboratory procedures and instrumentation. In the meantime, my responsibilities continued to grow. I remember coming home and telling my wife about my promotions, which were about every six months. I went from supervisor to assistant chief to chief technologist in fewer than four years. In my fifth year, I was promoted again to assistant manager of the laboratory. It was a real revelation since it meant being responsible for four departments. Besides being assistant manager of the Clinical Laboratory, Anatomical Pathology, and Nuclear Medicine, I now managed the Multiphasic program, a program where Kaiser was interested in preventative healthcare. A great idea, I thought. Kaiser San Francisco was, at the time, the only organization that began to provide this kind of program. I felt good about the fact that this program was receiving such recognition.

In 1972, in my sixth year at Kaiser Hospital in San Francisco, I was promoted to manager of the laboratory. It was a heavy load for several reasons—first, my office's location was in an area outside the laboratory. Second, there were two secretaries, and there was truly little room to accommodate them. Third, I dealt with personality issues with Dr. Basis and the Transcription department and the Cytology department.

To the best of my knowledge, our family life was improving. My wife worked at Fromm and Sisal, distributors of Christian Brothers wine. We now had two cars, and it was easier to get around. Beverly was attending Westborough Middle School and was soon to start El Camino High School in Daly City.

By now, I was getting closer to getting my master's degree

in clinical science from San Francisco State University and a master's from Central Michigan University. These postgraduate degrees did not come easy. There were many hours of taking classes both on campus and outside of traditional school systems. My first postgraduate degree was in clinical sciences. I had accumulated over two hundred units at San Francisco State University while also working full time at Kaiser San Francisco.

Chapter 72

MY FIRST POST-GRADUATE DEGREE

THE MAJOR CHALLENGE for receiving my MS in clinical science was the selection of a committee. I had decided to give an oral thesis presentation. My first graduate degree committee was Dr. Milton Basis, Dr. Jack Coppenger, Dr. Claude Alexander, and Dr. Ken Bayliss, I took two weeks off from work to prepare for the oral thesis exam. It was challenging to prepare for such an exam, particularly since the committee members would ask questions based on their specialty. Of course, the questions that they would ask were unknown to me. Thus, I had to pass this exam on pathology, endocrinology, parasitology, and statistics questions. Also, this would be my first such challenge.

I remember going to school that day feeling comfortable. We all met in one of the classrooms, where I was in front of this highly qualified group of people. Each one of the committee members was to ask a question, and I had to answer. I was very nervous, and the first question was on endocrinology. I was shaking and had difficulty responding to the question. The chair of the committee asked me to go outside and take a few minutes to compose myself. I stepped outside of the room and had a cup of coffee, and smoked a cigarette, as I recall. After a few minutes, I returned to the room and felt comfortable responding to the questions. After answering the first question, I began to feel comfortable and started to answer questions by each member of the committee in their specialty. The questioning went on for over an hour, and I felt confident that I was doing well. In fact, except for one question in endocrinology that I had difficulty answering, all the rest were entirely satisfactory. After this session, I felt confident that I had passed the oral exam for my master's in clinical science.

My second master's was in management and supervision of healthcare workers from Central Michigan University. This unique type of program required one to sign up in advance for the required classes. Before attending the one-week class held in different cities in the United States, we would get our material to study, so we would have a good idea of what to expect when we arrived for the class. It was a very intense program, and to get credits, we would take one or two quizzes and a final examination. The program was called an Open University, and it was all given without ever attending the university campus.

I was then working as the manager of Kaiser Foundation Hospital, and there was very little time for socializing. Monica Armstrong, my secretary, had a good education. She was an outstanding secretary and was very capable of all of the administrative aspects of laboratory functions. I had selected Monica over Zeobana because of her ability and her university education.

Monica's writing skills were excellent. After completing some of my papers, she would help type them, which was helpful since I did not know how to use the typewriter.

Monica was married but did not have any children. It was clear that she had marital issues and things were difficult for her. Regarding her work, it was well done. We both had to share the same office, and at times, it was difficult for me to deal with employee issues while she was present. I needed privacy when the employee required problems to a resolution. It also became evident that she liked me very much, which created problems for me. I found it exceedingly difficult to manage the laboratory department and to share the office with my secretary. However, it had to do, as there was no other solution.

Chapter 73

TARA, OUR SECOND CHILD

WHEN MARIKA HAD moved back in with us for the second time, Alexandra expected our little Tara. Tara, our second child, was born at Kaiser in San Francisco in April 1970. Beverly was nine years old at the time.

It may seem like a long time to wait to have another child, but some external factors were at play. Alexandra and I had to wait due to our immigration status as well as our financial situation. My wife and I had to work and go to school simultaneously since we were still on student visas. Another reason was that while my wife was pregnant, she decided to visit Greece to attend her sister's wedding. While she was there, she had a miscarriage. It was a tough time for me since I was not there with her. I wanted to visit her while she was in Greece, but due to financial constraints, this was not possible.

I remember the day when Tara arrived in this world. Since I had to work while my wife was in the delivery room, I would go up to the Labor and Delivery department to check on my little one's arrival. Things were different these days since we were not allowed to be in the delivery rooms. Tara arrived at around ten AM, and I remember visiting the nursery to see her. She was a beautiful baby. I also called my wife, and both were doing simply fine.

Chapter 74

NEW BABY AT HOME

MARIKA STAYING WITH us at our home in Daly City was fortunate for us while my wife was at the hospital. Beverly had started her schooling, and Marika greeted her when she came home from school. Marika was a great help during this period in our life. She was welcome to stay as long as necessary, but Marika felt she had to find a job and make a life for herself. It was a challenge since she did not have the required credentials or command of the English language. Since I was the manager of the Kaiser Foundation Hospital's laboratory, I decided to hire her. I had her start as a phlebotomy trainee. She was a fast learner and quickly became a phlebotomist. Soon she had a full-time job working as a phlebotomist with a similar schedule as mine. We would drive together from Daly City to San Francisco during the week. Marika learned quickly and soon understood all aspects of phlebotomy procedures. Having accomplished such a program, I promoted her to laboratory assistant 111. Being a laboratory assistant 111 allowed her to make better money, and, of course, if needed, she could fill in both areas as required. Her coworkers included some of the resident pathology doctors who much liked Marika. One of the resident pathologists showed great interest and began to take her on dates from our home in Daly City.

Marika's mother arrived in 1971. While Marika lived with us, her father and brother lived in Berkeley. Mr. Mataras, Marika's father, worked in a restaurant in Berkeley, while Paul went to Berkeley High School. After Mrs. Mataras arrived, they moved to 18th Avenue in San Francisco, and I got Paul a job in the laboratory as well. Mr. Mataras continued to work in Berkeley while Paul worked at San Francisco Kaiser. It was good to see the family live together, but this was not to last for very long. Marika decided to move out and find an apartment near Kaiser, and there was no issue with transportation due to the proximity.

Chapter 75

MASTER'S IN MANAGEMENT

IT TOOK ME two years to complete my master's degree in management. I was allowed to transfer up to thirty units from my masters in clinical science from San Francisco State University. Once I had obtained two graduate degrees, I felt relieved and comfortable in my leadership role at the Clinical Laboratory and within science. With this in hand, my position was secure, and I also thought that the hospital administration had more respect for me. I was part of an administrative team that gave me some leeway to make day-to-day decisions. I was also among a few who were on a long-range planning team.

Working for the Kaiser organization was unique, because it is one of the best health maintenance organizations (HMOs) in the United States. This system has a two-pronged approach to providing healthcare within a community. The first is the Kaiser Foundation health plan. Under this system, one must purchase health insurance through the Kaiser Foundation Hospital. The second is the physician group. The physicians can only practice medicine within Kaiser hospitals and cannot see patients unless they have a health plan membership. One of the essential strategies under such a plan is to contain costs while maintaining quality. It was a unique system, and I felt good to have started in such a system.

Kaiser eventually experimented with accepting solo-practice and group-practice physicians who were not a part of the Permanente Medical Group, which led them to purchase Santa Theresa Hospital in San Jose.

When an opportunity came for a position in the laboratory in San Jose, I applied for that position and got hired as the laboratory manager at the Santa Theresa facility. The opportunity inspired me to gain experience in a hybrid Kaiser system. The administration and the medical team were pleased to have me. At the time, we lived in Daly City, and I had to commute to San Jose every weekday. It was an awfully long commute, and it was tough on me. In addition to the commute, the laboratory technologists went on strike three months after I started. It created a challenge for me, as I had to learn how to perform laboratory testing again. Most automated technologies were easy to relearn, though the most challenging machine to learn was the SMA 12/60. The chemistry analyzer produced twelve chemistry results. Since I had never operated this instrument before, I had to call a friend at St. Mary's Hospital and get a quick one-on-one orientation to perform the test.

It was a tough time for me during this strike, as I had to adjust to the new facility and perform routine laboratory testing on a twenty-four-hour basis. There were times when I had to stay at the hospital for three days straight. After working and managing the facility during this challenging time, I would try to come home for a day, but along the way, I had to stop on the roadside to rest before coming home. Upon arriving home, my wife and kids wanted to spend time with me, but I could not respond to their needs. It was tough for me. My wife was very sympathetic but felt she needed to do something so I did not commute to San Jose.

She had seen an advertisement for a position at Mary's Help Hospital in Daly City. My resume was sent to the hospital without my knowledge by my wife. The management requested to interview me for the laboratory manager's position: I was interviewed by Dr. Thomas Bruce, the other pathologists, and the hospital's assistant administrator. I also met Chito Balan, the chief technologist of the laboratory. After a few weeks of waiting, I got the manager position. It was challenging to make the decision, but I accepted the job because of my commuting concerns.

Then came the time to submit my resignation to Santa Theresa Hospital. Mr. Sweeney, the hospital administrator, was my boss. He already knew of my intention to resign and made the process much easier for me. Mr. Sweeney took me to lunch to talk it over. He informed me that the physician-in-chief of Santa Clara Kaiser, Dr. Brown, knew Dr. Thomas Bruce, who had called to ask about me. It became apparent that Dr. Bruce had requested a reference check on me without my knowledge. Dr. Brown had given Dr. Bruce a very glowing recommendation about me. Thus, I was offered the position at Mary's Help Hospital. Here I was sweating talking to my boss about my desire to leave this excellent facility and my twelve years of service to the Kaiser Foundation Hospital. Still, the leadership of the hospital had known of my intention all along. It was a sad day for me to say goodbye to the administration and the laboratory staff, who had been very nice to me.

Chapter 76

NEW BEGINNING

FINALLY, THE DAY arrived when I reported to work at Mary's Help Hospital, on September 18, 1978. Because of my position as a hospital-based laboratory manager, I had to be oriented by Miss Marie Mahoney. Marie Mahoney, a very highly regarded person at the hospital, was close to the administration and all the nuns who worked at the hospital. Marie spent the entire day with me to ensure that I understood the Daughters of Charity Health System and its history. I also received a tour of the hospital and the chapel, which was within the hospital. The Daughters of Charity, a Catholic organization, had a head office in Saint Louis, Missouri. At the time, this organization had several hospitals in various states throughout the United States. They also had up to six hospitals and clinics in California. Mary's Help Hospital, located in Daly City, California, was next to the I-280 freeway.

My second day of work was very hectic. I did not realize how challenging the situation was in the Clinical Laboratory, Pathology department, and Nuclear Medicine department. The chief technologist was very welcoming and was trying to manage the Clinical Laboratory and Pathology department. It became apparent to me very quickly some of the significant issues facing the departments. The previous manager had already left, which meant that I had to learn independently—for example, the monthly administrative reports required manual labor. I had no idea where to get started.

I had to call the previous manager to get the answers; she arranged to meet me at a restaurant in San Rafael to help me out, but she never showed up. There was no one to provide the support that I needed. In addition to management issues, I soon discovered staffing issues and personnel problems. One of the night shift employees took it upon himself to change our chief Technologist's already posted schedule. I had to confront him on numerous occasions about this and a few other issues. He continued to do his own thing. After a discussion with Human Resources, I had to suspend him for a few days. Of course, he was not happy about this. A couple of days later, I was having breakfast with the assistant manager of the Human Resources department at the cafeteria on the second floor of the hospital building. This person came in and confronted me while I was having breakfast in front of other personnel. He uttered a few choice words and proceeded to give me a sermon. After he left the building, I discussed this incident with the director of Human Resources, and we agreed to end his employment with Mary's Help Hospital. Of course, he did not accept the news well, so he sued the hospital and me—the actual first challenge for me at this new facility. The case dragged on for around a year. The outcome was that we won the case, and he ended up paying the hospital some money. I am not sure if the hospital got any cash collected.

The second issue at the facility was in the Nuclear Medicine department. The supervisor in the department was challenging to manage. He was a drama queen and constantly created problems with his staff as well as with physicians. I had to have a few discussions with him but to no avail. One of the major problems was the receptionist, who supported him fully. Because the department was somewhat of a distance from my office, managing the department was a huge challenge. My office was in the Clinical Laboratory. I soon realized that some issues were confronting me. After I reviewed a few procedures, it became apparent that the laboratory had been poorly managed for a few years. So, I had to apply a few management principles to keep me sane and surviving.

Being trained at Kaiser and equipped with a master's in management was extremely helpful. The first thing that I did was create an organizational chart. With this in hand, the lines of responsibilities were made very apparent. The second thing that I did was establish a regular weekly meeting with our pathologist, the chief technologists, and myself. The third thing I did was to have regular monthly meetings with the staff. Finally, the fourth thing was to meet with my boss weekly to get his support for my efforts.

Working at Mary's Help Hospital was vastly different from Kaiser. The difference between the two organizations was huge. Even though both hospitals took care of patients, there was a fundamental difference. At Kaiser hospitals, the patients were on insurance plans; thus, they did not have to pay for services received or they paid minimal fees while registering for a service. At Mary's Help Hospital, patients had to pay for services received. Managing costs within the Kaiser system was much more critical than it was with Mary's Help Hospital.

The patient-physician relationship was very different as well. Besides learning how to manage at a new laboratory, I discovered another way of addressing financial and labor relations issues.

It was not difficult, but learning a different management system was challenging, especially with economic management. There were moments when I needed help, but there was no one to provide any support. I was on my own. The term sink-or-swim was very appropriate for me during this time. Within a few months, I had finally learned the system, and everything was proceeding.

My family and I were getting better at managing our finances and were ready to buy a better home and move away from Daly City. The most important consideration was to move to a location that would provide the best environment for our two daughters. Beverly was still at El Camino High School, but little Tara needed to attend a better school system. We began to look around for a better neighborhood and a better investment for our future. We found a real estate agent who was very helpful in showing us homes around Burlingame, San Mateo, and Hillsborough. We also looked at houses in south San Francisco. We almost bought a property in south San Francisco but decided not to take the deal, which ended up costing us a few dollars. We then found a home in Hillsborough, but it was costly, and financing was complex.

Fortunately, my wife had a helping hand from Mr. Fromm, the owner of Fromm & Sichel, who distributed Christian Brothers Wine. Mr. Fromm advanced us the down payment for the home in Hillsborough. It was not easy, but things began to look better. We were able to sell our home in Daly City and thus pay back Mr. Fromm within six months. We moved to Hillsborough in December, 1978. It was a great relief to move there. First, Hillsborough is a very exclusive town with some wealthy people. Secondly, this is a place many dream of coming to live for several reasons. But for us, the most important reason was for our children. Tara started South School, which was rated as among the top ten percent of schools in the country. Tara had a challenging time adjusting from the Daly City school system to the Hillsborough school system. More importantly, just the change from one school to another was a difficult adjustment to make for a six-year-old. It was excruciating for her mother to leave her crying at the school, even though the teachers assured her that Tara would be all right and that she should leave her with them.

Beverly attended the University of California, Berkeley, and moved to Berkeley to complete her undergraduate studies. Beverly adjusted well. One of the reasons was that she had already attended San Francisco State University and transferred into the UC system. Beverly initially seemed to get along well, but later we found out that adjusting presented some trouble. She did well and finally did graduate from this school. After completing her BA in political science, we were proud to see her going to Hastings Law School. Beverly faced this new challenge, but she graduated from Hastings with a JD (Juris Doctor). It was indeed a proud moment for our family and me to see her receive a well-deserved credential. There was a big graduation ceremony at the auditorium in downtown San Francisco. We also had a lovely celebration for Beverly and her friends at our home in Hillsborough.

Getting a law degree is one thing, but passing the California Bar Exam is another. Beverly was able to pass the California Bar on her first try. Not a small feat. We were thrilled to see her accomplish all this in just a few years. After her graduation, she decided to take a trip to Australia. It was a gift from us, and we were happy to be able to do it. Upon her return, she found a job in Los Angeles with a highly reputable firm. We were extremely excited for her; however, it was sad that she would be leaving the Bay Area and her family for a job in Los Angeles. Our family had always been together here in the Bay Area and to face this separation was a challenging moment for us. I remember driving down to Los Angeles and finding a decent apartment for her. Of course, Beverly was excited about starting her career with the new law firm. As a new attorney and in a completely unfamiliar environment, we were concerned about her welfare but realized that she would be fine. Since her interest was entertainment law, it was in the right environment. She met her future husband there, and before too long, we had a wonderful wedding here at a Greek church in San Francisco. After the wedding, the spouses went back to Los Angeles. Sasha, our granddaughter, arrived, and we were delighted to have our first grandchild. Fortunately, we were with Beverly in the delivery room when our little Sasha came. She was a beautiful little girl, and we were delighted that she was strong and healthy. Beverly named her Sasha Karan Narayan after my father and me. It was exceptional to have a granddaughter who was named Sasha Karan Narayan.

While life kept changing for me, Beverly and her family decided to move back to the Bay Area. Since they had no place to stay, they moved in with us. We welcomed the idea since now we could spend some precious time with our granddaughter Sasha. Beverly started to work for a firm in Redwood City, while Jimmy, her husband, was challenged finding a job. Home Depot finally hired him; the poor person had to work extremely hard since he had worked in parts distribution in Los Angeles. Jimmy was interested in music and dedicated most of his time to his love of music. We realized that this would not work while having a family. So, I suggested that he begin to go to junior college and start a program in Computer Science. He followed this plan, but the music was his first love, and he continued to find time for it.

After a year with us, they found an apartment in San Mateo on 3rd Avenue not too far from our home. While they were in this apartment, our second granddaughter arrived. We were delighted to have Kaiya in our life. Kaiya Maria Narayan was such a joy. There was such a difference between the two granddaughters. They are four years apart and have different looks as well as different personalities. Once Kaiya arrived, the apartment manager began to comment on the kids and did not want them at the apartment anymore. Once I learned about this, I immediately suggested that they buy a house. It was a welcome relief for our family. They moved to their new home on Howard Avenue in Burlingame.

After a few years, Beverly and Jimmy filed for divorce, and life for the kids changed. I was not incredibly pleased with this situation and began to support our grandkids in any way that I could. The most important thing was that their grandmother quit her job to be available for the grandkids. It was terrific for our family since their grandmother would provide both Sasha and Kaiya with security and love. Parents who have gone through a separation must appreciate life's challenges, especially when the father of my grandchildren was not supportive. To make the situation worse, he demanded settlement payments from Beverly. With the money he received from her, he immediately bought a house in Pacifica. He insisted on having the kids once per week, especially over the weekend, when Beverly could have spent some precious time with her children. He continued to make life for my daughter difficult. I am thankful, however, that we were there to provide support to our grandchildren whenever they needed any assistance.

Tara, our younger daughter, remained in San Mateo and was working part-time as she attended San Francisco State University. After graduating from the university in 1992, she went to work at The Gap. Working for an established company was an opportunity for learning marketing and a way for her to become efficient in her chosen field. Tara was a fantastic child who was full of potential to excel in marketing and sales. She is a gifted leader and will someday be managing a department of her own.

I have always believed in ensuring that my children and grandchildren need to be independent and self-confident in their futures as women. They should never rely on anyone for support, and they must make a living on their terms. When they have children, they need to be prepared to support them. I am very proud to say that my daughters can manage independently and do not have to rely on support from anyone.

After ensuring that my daughters were getting the proper education and experiences in their lives, I began to consider going back to school to complete my doctorate. Since my background was in science, it was vital for me to get another credential in management. I wanted to learn as much as I could and manage the Laboratory department to the best of my ability. I am a firm believer in being the best that I can be when an opportunity comes along my way. I must admit that I have seen many pretend to be leaders but who do not promote themselves to become good leaders.

Chapter 77

RESEARCH PROJECT *for* PHD: NEVER TOO OLD *for* EDUCATION

WHEN BEVERLY COMPLETED her law degree, it was a joy since I wanted a lawyer in our family. It was because of my brother, Ravindra, who had passed away too soon. He had gone to New Zealand to study law while I had to stay on the farm after completing class eight. His death was devastating to our family. I did not learn of his death until after a month had elapsed. No one from Fiji told us that he had passed away. In those days, communication from Fiji to the States was abysmal. It is significant to note that our family in the village did not have a telephone to call us, nor any convenient means to keep us informed. Ramesh and Bhupendra were also in California with me. We grieved for Ravindra's death, but we had to continue living our lives since every day was a challenge to make a living. In any case, it was important to me that we had another lawyer in our family.

After Beverly completed her education, I finally saw an opportunity to start my doctorate program. Indeed, it was a challenging decision to make since I was working full-time at Seton Medical Center. But with support from my wife, I decided to sign up for a PhD program at Cappella University. The university, located in Minnesota, is close to the University of Minnesota. The school dean was no other than the same person at Central Michigan University, where I had completed my master's in management and supervision for healthcare workers. The application process was not complex since I already had two master's degrees. I was accepted to the PhD program in June of 1996 without much issue. The school received a transfer of up to thirty units of credit from my two master's programs, which meant that all I needed to complete would be thirty additional academic units.

The most challenging part of the program was to select a research project of PhD caliber. I decided to choose my project at Seton Medical Center in Disease Management and Preventive Care. Specifically, I felt that we needed to open a clinic where patients from the local community could get blood samples drawn to perform blood glucose analysis to test for diabetes. The second test was a lipid profile for cardiovascular disease. The third part of the program was to achieve blood pressure tests for hypertension. The idea was to have patients access a local hospital laboratory where licensed and trained healthcare workers could assist as needed. A qualified phlebotomist would be available to draw blood from the patient during the morning hours. The sample would be then processed for lipid profile and blood sugar tests by a licensed technologist. The clinic would accept patients from seven in the morning to noon, once per month on Sundays.

I initially started to check for blood pressure, but this became difficult because those patients with high blood pressure needed special attention, which meant they had to go to ER. Our ER docs found it unacceptable that we sent patients with high blood pressure to the ER. I had to drop this part of the program. I found an easy solution since anyone can have their blood pressure checked at any local pharmacy. Also, it is easy to buy a blood pressure machine at a very reasonable cost for home use.

I also developed a simple form to check for three risk categories for diabetes, cardiovascular disease, and hypertension. This form, when used properly, can identify those who are at high risk for the three chronic conditions of my interest. I attended the clinic on Sundays and made sure that all was going as planned. I also met the patients and helped answer any questions they had. The patients would come to the clinic and complete a registration form, and on an envelope, they would write their address for us to mail the results directly to them. After completing the registration and blood draw, a phlebotomist would take the specimen for testing. After performing the test, we would send the result directly to the patient. I was able to complete the research program within four years.

The second phase of the program was to complete the thirty units. The school had several professors who specialized in up to twenty different subjects. In addition to this, I would select a mentor for my dissertation. I chose my mentor, who had a PhD in psychology and humanities. I had to take two weeks off from work and attend the campus for proper orientation to get started. For these two weeks, we met most of the professors and the students on the campus at a local college. We had a great introduction to various aspects of how to proceed and the selection of our research projects. Those in attendance received three units toward meeting the curriculum requirement.

Upon my return home, I had to sign up for my subjects, which would lead to me completing the program in Interdisciplinary Studies. Interdisciplinary Studies made sense since I already had a master's in management and a second masters in clinical science. My title selection appeared appropriate since I was a director of the Clinical Laboratory, Pathology, Nuclear Medicine, Radiology, and Radiation Oncology departments at Seton Medical Center. To complete the required number of units, I had to design a routine while working full time during weekdays. I also often had to work during weekends, which meant less time to focus on my studies.

On Monday through Friday, I would go to work around seven-thirty in the morning. After working for eight-plus hours each day, I would come home and, after family time, eat dinner and go to sleep around eight in the evening. I would sleep till about twelve-thirty AM and would get up to study until three in the morning. Then I would go back to sleep, wake up by six in the morning, and get ready to work. My wife would be up to make my breakfast and my lunch to take to work.

On the weekends, I would set aside most Saturdays and Sundays for studies and completing my homework. For each class, I had to write a paper on a specific subject. In all of the lessons that I took except for one type, I looked forward to completing the research papers promptly. The one class that was a challenge was due to the professor's unwillingness to accept my position. The most comprehensive article that I wrote was on my research on the beginning of religion. This paper fascinated me. I also researched the human condition, psychology, teenage suicide, the biological basis of behavior, and more.

After three years of following this routine, I decided to take a vacation with my wife, and we went to Greece for two weeks. Upon our return from Greece, I finally completed the course that gave me the most challenging time. I barely passed this class, which was the last one toward achieving the thirty units.

Once I was able to complete the required thirty units, I began to focus on writing my dissertation. After I collected the appropriate data, I was able to write it. The data that I collected showed that disease management and preventive care were successful and very practical. Few hospitals, clinics, or pharmacies did anything concerning these areas when I began this program. Once the program got established, facilities adopted the idea and provided direct patient care using my system. California extended the testing to include broader testing menus that did not require a physician order. Before getting started on the dissertation, I needed to form a committee. The committee's responsibility would be to review the dissertation and approve it before sending it to the school. I was delighted to complete and receive the proper approval. Once the school got the dissertation, it had to be audited for the correctness and appropriate English grammar; when this was complete, I got the copy back. I had to retype and resubmit it for publication. The school published three copies of the dissertation. They kept one as a copy for their library, and I received two copies. I was proud to complete the program with extremely high marks from the dissertation committee. I was to go to Minnesota to receive my doctorate degree in June 2000. Alexandra and our two daughters were able to attend my graduation. I was getting my PhD which was indeed a proud moment for my family and me. Finally, I was able to complete my dream. At my first meeting at the hospital, the administrative team helped celebrate my accomplishment. Additionally, I was honored with an article in our monthly newsletter. Many were amazed by what I had accomplished while working full-time at Seton Medical Center in Daly City.

I was now Dr. Jay Narayan at work. My life at work continued with not much change either in pay or in any special recognition. I remained as the director of the Clinical Laboratory, Pathology, Radiology, Nuclear Medicine, and Radiation Oncology departments for the remainder of my tenure at Seton Medical Center. When I turned sixty-five years of age, it was time to take my retirement. My boss was happy for me.

However, the president and chief operating officer requested that I stay but work only part-time. Part of the reason was that I was also responsible for the hazardous materials management program. I was fully qualified for such a position. It was because of having a certificate in this field from the University of California at Berkeley. To put this in a proper perspective, it took me two and a half years to get a certificate. I was required to attend classes on Fridays and Saturdays every week. After taking all the required courses and passing all the exams, I received the certificate. I spent two days a week attending classes for the UC Extension Program to get this certificate. Most of the classes were in downtown San Francisco. I would take a BART train from San Mateo to San Francisco. Some of the classes were in Walnut Creek, and in this situation, I had to drive. These classes were all day long, and it was not easy to make this happen. I did this while working full-time at Seton Medical Center. This program came under a unique project for the hospital, of which I took advantage.

Once equipped with the knowledge of hazardous materials management, I developed safety programs for Seton Medical Center and Seton Medical Center Coast Side. After being on this unique project for two years, the administration decided to eliminate the position. The irony is, and this is true in many aspects of our lives, that anyone with minimal knowledge can occupy a post without proper education. I have been surprised at the hospital inspecting agencies that willingly accept officers with minimal understanding of such essential safety issues. It is no wonder some severe incidents occur, and lives are lost when we do not address the issue of concern. I had to retire from Seton Medical Center in 2007. The program was never the same. It is sad to say, but the reality is that life does go on, and the organizations tolerate the acceptance of mediocrity.

APPENDIX

FAMILY TREE

BADAL
(Great Grandfather)

RAM PHAL
(Grandfather)

CHANGI
(Mother)

DEO NARAYAN
(Brother)

JAI NARAYAN
(Brother)

SHIU NARAYAN
(Brother)

CHANDRA KUMARI
(Sister)

SHIU KUMAR
(Brother)

RAVINDRA NATH
(Brother)

UTRA KUMARI
(Sister)

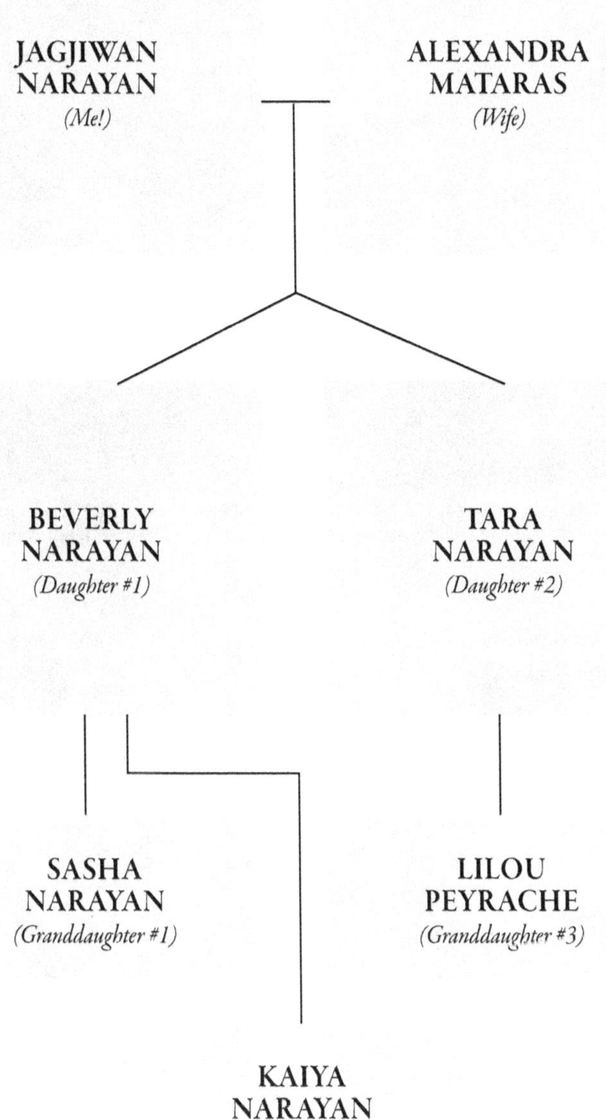
JAGJIWAN
NARAYAN
(Me!)
ALEXANDRA
MATARAS
(Wife)
BEVERLY
NARAYAN
(Daughter #1)
TARA
NARAYAN
(Daughter #2)
SASHA
NARAYAN
(Granddaughter #1)
LILOU
PEYRACHE
(Granddaughter #3)
KAIYA
NARAYAN
(Granddaughter #2)

PHOTOGRAPHS

My father

From left to right, top row: My Father Jai Karan, brother-in-law Narayan Dutt, Uncles Ram Prasad, Harry Prasad, & Bechu Prasad. Bottom row: Mausa Girwar Sing, Jahajibhai, Nana Ram Phal and Bal Gobind

Mother Changi

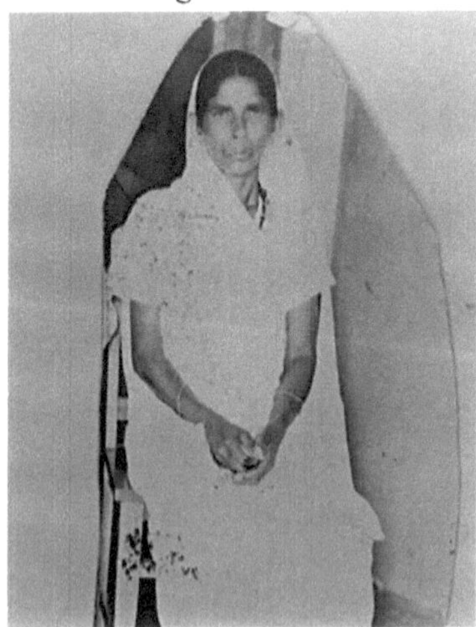

My dearest Mother Changi

Brother Deo Narayan, oldest son of Mother Changi, with his wife.

Me with Master Jai Narayan of Jai Narayan College, Suva, Fiji. Second son of Mother Changi

Back row: Shiu Narayan, third son of Mother Changi with his wife on his left. Father Jai Karan and in front of him my chotki and Badki Mom. Sister Kamla, to my mother Changi's left and her left is Mrs. and Mr. Brother Deo Narayan with the family children. The family was at the Nadi Airport to see me depart from Fiji for the USA.

My mother Changi's fourth son, Shiu Kumar, and his two children. Shiu Kumar Biganath went to Germany and became a doctor. On left is his daughter Chandra and his son Shusil.

My wife, Alexandra

Alexandra holding her two granddaughters, Sasha on the left and next to her is Kaiya. This picture was taken on Easter day at our home in Hillsborough.

Wedding picture of my first granddaughter, Sasha, with her husband, Yannis, in the middle. In front of Kaiya is me and my wife, Alexandra. To the left of the bride is my daughter Bev and next to her is my daughter Tara and Miss Lilou. Behind her is Loris and brother Luke.

Tara and Beverly Narayan, our precious daughters.

From left me and my Greek brothers-in-law, Chris and John

In the center is my granddaughter Kaiya and her husband, Charlie, newly married. From left in the back row is Loris and daughter Tara and Yannis and Dr. Jay. Front row from left is my wife, Alexandra, daughter Beverly and the married couple, Sasha, and Miss Lilou.

From left: my wife, Alexandra, her brother Dimitri, her father Mr. Mataras and her mother Alexandra. My precious family.

My sisters, Utra and Chandra.

Elaine on our wedding day

From left is Alexandra, Elaine and me. I lived with Elaine who looked after me during my junior college days. This our wedding picture in June 1960.

Elaine and I at the Richmond courthouse. This is the courthouse where Alexandra and I got married in Richmond, California.

From left is Brother Ramesh and in the middle is Brother Prem and next to him is Brother Ravindra Nath.

Irene and Jai Narayan

Master Jai Narayan of Jai Narayan College in Fiji and his wife, Irene Jai Narayan, first women in the Fiji Parliament.

Alexandra and me taking a tour on a ship.

Tara, my youngest daughter, with Lilou Peyrache, my youngest precious granddaughter.

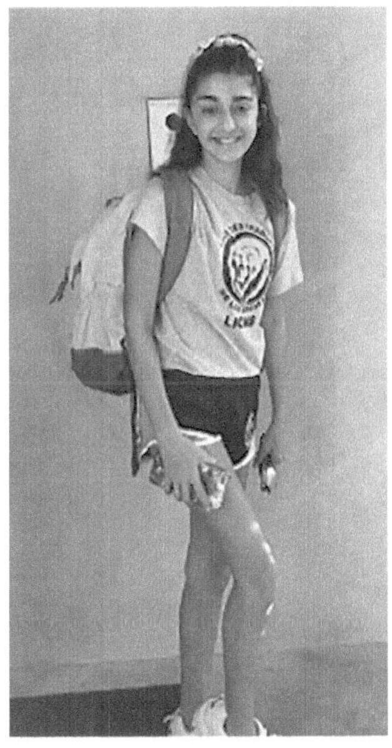

My youngest granddaughter Miss Lilou Peyrache ready for high school.

Sasha Karan Narayan MD. Graduation picture from Oregon Health and Science University Medical School and residency at Johns Hopkins Hospital.

Kaiya's graduation picture. A summa cum laude at Citadel, The Military College of South Carolina.

MAPS

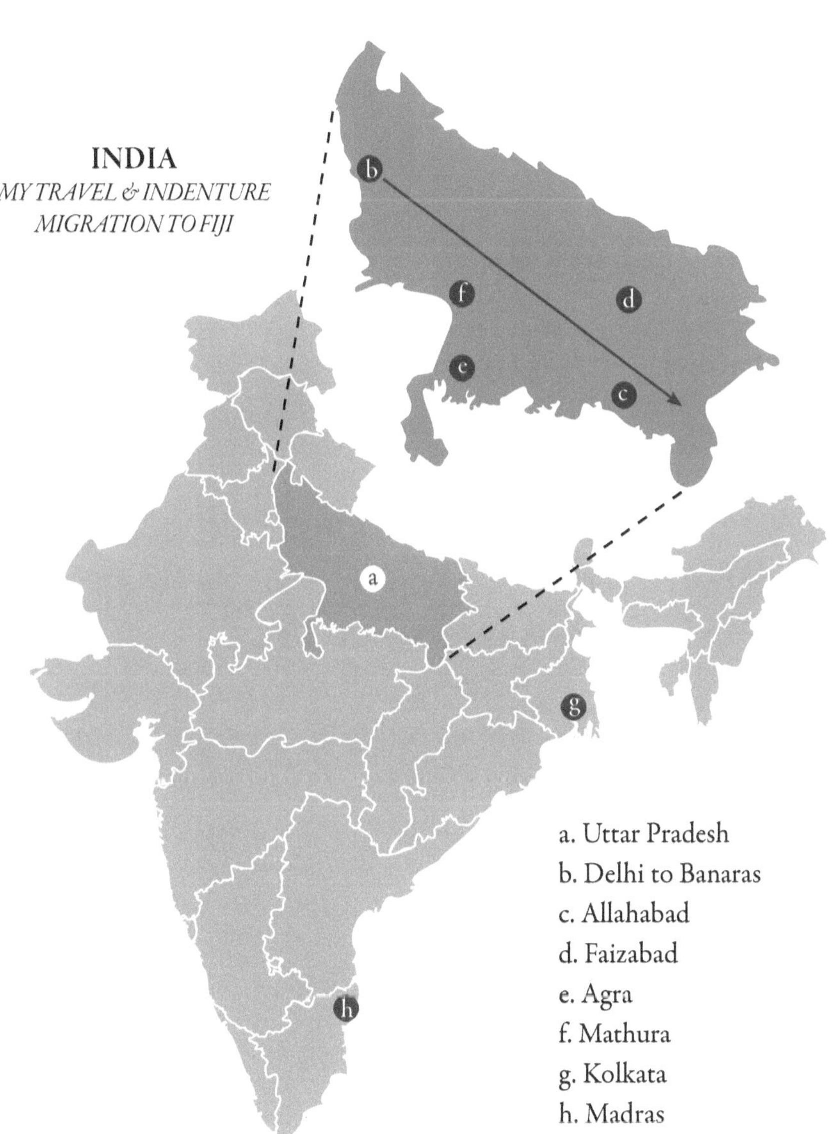
INDIA
MY TRAVEL & INDENTURE MIGRATION TO FIJI
a
b
c
c
d
e
f
g
h
a. Uttar Pradesh
b. Delhi to Banaras
c. Allahabad
d. Faizabad
e. Agra
f. Mathura
g. Kolkata
h. Madras

FIJI ISLANDS

INDENTURE SETTLEMENTS

b

d

c

a

a. Viti Levu
b. Vanua Levu
c. Taveuni
d. Turtle Islands

GREECE

MY WIFE'S FAMILY

a. Livadia
b. Athens
c. Pyerius

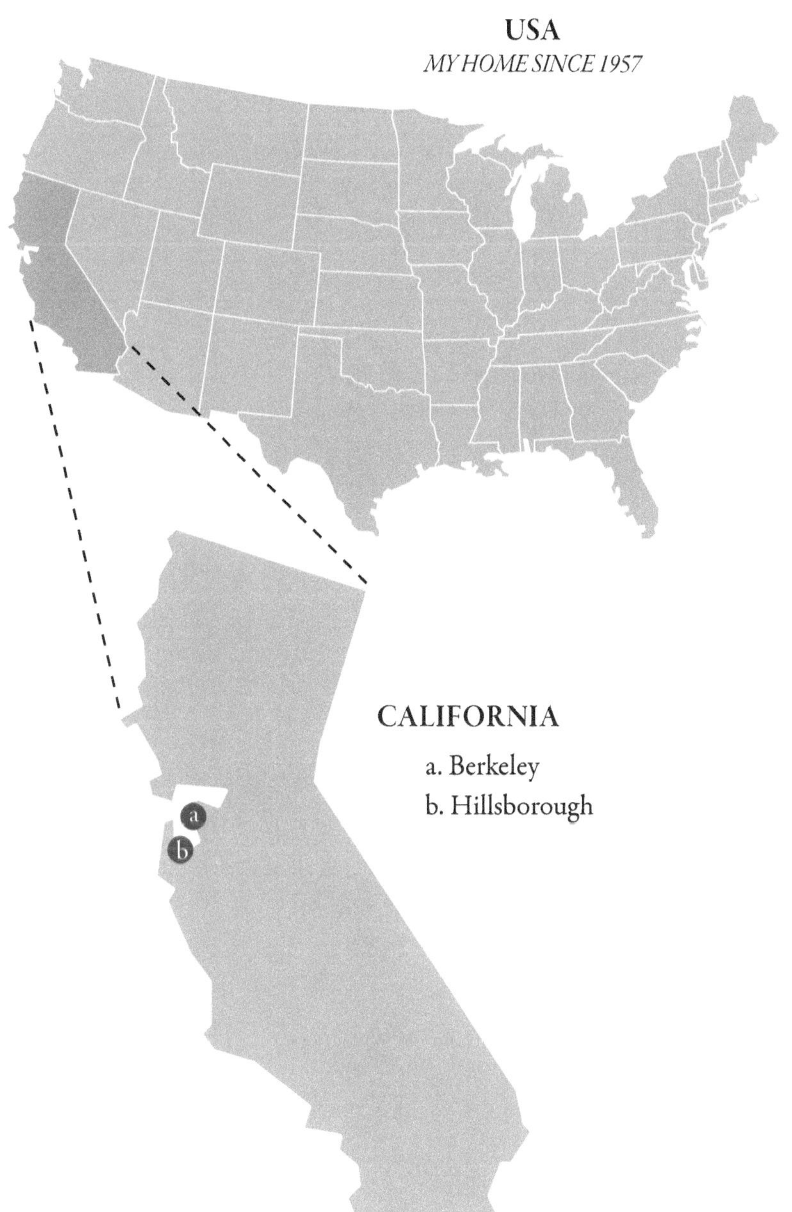
USA
MY HOME SINCE 1957
CALIFORNIA
a. Berkeley
b. Hillsborough
a
b

ENDNOTES

CHAPTER 1

1. Naidu, V., *Violence of Indenture in Fiji*. Page 1
2. Chaudhry, M., *Children of the Indus*. Page 7
3. Sanadhya, T., *My Twenty-One Years in the Fiji Islands*. Pages 1, 36, 37 & 46
4. Sharma, G.D., *Memories of Fiji 1887-1987*. Page 3
5. Sharma, N., "An Old Letter, a New Vision." I*ndia-Fiji Experiences to Remember*.
6. Sanadhya, T., *My Twenty-One Years in the Fiji Islands*.
7. Naidu, V., *Violence of Indenture in Fiji*. Page 13
8. Chaudhry, M., *Children of the Indus*.
9. Wood, M., *The Story of India*.
10. Ibid
11. Ibid
12. Sanadhya, T., *My Twenty-One Years in the Fiji Islands*. Page 36
13. Sharma, N., *India-Fiji*. Page 17
14. Sanadhya, T., *My Twenty-One Years in the Fiji Islands*.

CHAPTER 2

1. Prasad, R., *Tears in Paradise: Suffering and Struggles of Indians in Fiji 1879-2004*. Page 118
2. Wood, M., *India*. Page 37
3. Ibid, page 38
4. Sharma, G. D., *Memories of Fiji 1887-1987*.

CHAPTER 3

1. Sharma, G. D., *Memories of Fiji 1887-1987*. Page XI
2. Ibid
3. Robert, K., *Fiji: A Travel Survival Kit*.
4. Prasad, R., *Tears in Paradise*. Page 9
5. Chaudhry, M., *Children of the Indus*.
6. Chandra Gupta Maurya
7. Naidu, V., *Violence of Indenture in Fiji*. Pages 10 & 11
8. Naidu, V., *Violence of Indenture in Fiji*. Page 5
9. Sanadhya, T., Narak or hell
10. Joginder, K. S., India-Fiji.

CHAPTER 5

1. Gillion, K.L., *Fiji's Indian Migrants*. Page 30
2. Naidu, V., *Violence of Indenture in Fiji*. Page 15
3. Ibid, page 16

CHAPTER 7

1. Chaudhry, M., *Children of the Indus*.

CHAPTER 11

1. Sanadhya, T.,

CHAPTER 18

1. Sharma, G.D., *Memories of Fiji 1887-1987*. Page 164

BIBLIOGRAPHY

Ali, A. (1979). *Girmit : Indian indenture experience in Fiji.* Suva, Fiji: Fiji Museum.

Ali, A. (1980). *Plantation to Politics: Studies on Fiji Indian.* Suva, Fiji: University of the South Pacific, the Fiji Times & Herald Limited.

Bently, J. (1972). "Escape from Nukulau." *India-Fiji: Experiences to Remember.* Suva, Fiji: Indian Cultural Centre High Commission of India.

Brewster, D. A. (2010). *The Turtle and the Caduceus: How Pacific and Modern Medicine Shaped the Medical School in Fiji 1885-2010.* Xlibris Corporation.

Chandra, P. (1972). "Destiny." *India-Fiji: Experiences to Remember.* Suva, Fiji: Indian Cultural Centre High Commission of India Suva.

Chaudhry, M. (2004). *Children of the Indus.* National Farmers Union.

Gillion, K. L., Gillion, K. L. O. (1962). *Fiji's Indian Migrants: A History to the End of Indenture in 1920.* United Kingdom: Oxford University Press.

Jinna, K. (1972). "Ganga." *India-Fiji: Experiences to Remember.* Suva, Fiji: Indian Cultural Centre High Commission of India Suva.

Joginder, S. K. (1972). "Poetry: Girmit Grief." *India-Fiji: Experiences to Remember.* Suva, Fiji: Indian Cultural Centre High Commission of India Suva.

Kay, R. F. (1990). *Fiji: A Travel Survival Kit.* Lonely Planet Publication.

Kumar, V. (1972). "A Haven for Jahajis." *India-Fiji: Experiences to Remember*. Suva, Fiji: Indian Cultural Centre High Commission of India Suva.

Lal, V. B. (2000). *Chalo Jahaji on a Journey through indenture in Fiji*. Suva, Fiji: Division of Pacific & Asian Studies. Australia National University Canberra. Australia and Fiji Museum.

Mishra, K. K. (2013). *India-Fiji: Experiences to Remember*. Suva, Fiji: Indian Cultural Centre High Commission of India Suva.

Naidu, V. (2004). *The Violence of Indenture in Fiji*. Lautoka, Fiji: Fiji Institute of Applied Studies.

Nandan, K. I. (2005). *Stolen Words: Fiji Indian Fragments*. Ivy Press International.

Prasad, R. (2006). *Tears in Paradise: Unveiled Suffering and Struggle of Indians in Fiji 1879-2004*. Auckland, New Zealand: Glade Publishes.

Sanadhya, T. (2003). *My Twenty-One Years in the Fiji Islands & The Storage of the Haunted Line*. Suva, Fiji: Quality Print Limited.

Sharma, G. D. (1987). *Memories of Fiji 1887-1987*. Suva, Fiji: Fiji Times Ltd.

Sharma, N. (1972). "An Old Letter, a New Vision." *India-Fiji: Experiences to Remember*. Suva, Fiji: Indian Cultural Centre High Commission of India Suva.

Tikaram, M. (1972). "A Visit to India." *India-Fiji: Experiences to Remember*. Suva, Fiji: Indian Cultural Centre High Commission of India Suva.

Wood, M. (2007). *The Story of India*. Woodland Books Limited.

Yee, N. (2013). *Catching the Wind: A Search for God*. Xlibris.

JAY NARAYAN, Ph.D.

Hillsborough, CA

EDUCATION

A.A. Associate in Arts, 1963 – Contra Costa Junior College

B.A. Biological Science, 1966 – San Francisco State University

M.S. Clinical Science, 1976 – San Francisco State University

M.A. Management and Supervision, 1975 – Central Michigan University

Ph.D. Interdisciplinary Studies, 2000 – Capella University

PROFESSIONAL EXPERIENCE

SETON MEDICAL CENTER, DALY CITY, CALIFORNIA

DIRECTOR 2003-2007
Clinical laboratory, pathology, nuclear medicine, radiology, and radiation oncology.

ADMINISTRATIVE DIRECTOR 1985-2002
Clinical laboratory, pathology, nuclear medicine.

LABORATORY MANAGER 1978-1984

SANTA THERESA HOSPITAL

LABORATORY MANAGER 1977-1978

KAISER HOSPITAL, SAN FRANCISCO, CALIFORNIA

LABORATORY MANAGER 1973-1977

MEDICAL TECHNOLOGY INTERN 1966-1967

LICENSURE & CERTIFICATION

Clinical Laboratory Scientist, CLS 1966 – California Department of Health Services

Medical Technologist, MT (ASCP) 1966 – National Board Certified

Hazardous Materials Management, HMM, 1994 – University of California, Berkeley Extension

PUBLICATIONS

Narayan, J. Benefits of Chemistry Workstation Consolidation. Advance for Administrators of the Laboratory, July-August 1995, 1.

Narayan, J. Managing Cost. Advance for Administrators of the Laboratory, November 1995, 23-27.

RESEARCH INTEREST

My dissertation was on disease management and preventative care. I am interested in three specific chronic diseases: coronary artery disease, hypertension, and diabetes. I established an outpatient clinic at Seton Medical Center for lipid profile and diabetes that has been in operation since 1996.

HOBBIES

Gardening, golf, family and travel.

www.ingramcontent.com/pod-product-compliance
Lightning Source LLC
Chambersburg PA
CBHW020433130626
46549CB00001B/112
* 9 7 9 8 9 8 5 5 7 3 7 0 1 *